EXPOSITORY STUDIES IN ROMANS 9-16

A **DISCOVERY** **BIBLE STUDY** **BOOK**

EXPOSITORY STUDIES IN ROMANS 9-16

FROM GUILT TO GLORY
VOLUME II

RAY C. STEDMAN

WORD BOOKS
PUBLISHER
4800 WEST WACO DRIVE
WACO, TEXAS
76703

From Guilt to Glory,
Volume 2 (Romans 9–16)

Discovery Books are published by Word Books, Publisher, in
cooperation with Discovery Foundation, Palo Alto California.

ISBN 0–8499–2841–9
Library of Congress Catalog Card Number: 77–92460

Printed in the United States of America

Contents

1. Has God Failed? 9
2. Let God Be God 22
3. How to Be Saved 34
4. Have They Not Heard? 46
5. There's Hope Ahead 59
6. Our Great and Glorious God 71
7. Living Day by Day 81
8. Who Am I, Lord? 93
9. How to Hug 106
10. God's Strange Servants 117
11. The Night Is Nearly Over 128
12. On Trying to Change Others 139
13. The Right to Yield 151
14. Our Great Example 160
15. An Adequate Ministry 169
16. All in the Family 182
17. The Great Mystery 196
An Expanded Outline of Romans 205

EXPOSITORY STUDIES IN ROMANS 9-16

1

Has God Failed?

There is a verse in the Book of Jeremiah that comes to mind in connection with the ninth chapter of Romans. On one occasion when Jeremiah was very troubled about some things that were happening to him, he came to God and told him how he felt. Instead of comforting him, as he thought the Lord would do, the Lord said to him, "If you have fainted when you run with footmen, how will you contend with horses?" (Jer. 12:5). So if we had difficulty handling Paul's arguments in chapters 1 through 8 of Romans, what are we going to do now that we are in the ninth chapter? For in this chapter the apostle brings before us some of the toughest questions ever faced by man as he contemplates the actions and workings of God. All the bitter and denunciatory accusations that man ever brings against God are faced squarely in this chapter.

Chapters 1 through 8, the first major division of the letter, contain Paul's explanation of the gospel of the grace of God, the full plan of redemption. In the second division, chapters 9 through 11, the apostle seems to start all over again. He has been talking about the grace of God and has explained the gospel of God, and now he goes back over it again. But this time his purpose is not to explain the gospel, but to exhibit it. These chapters are an exhibition of the grace that takes man from terrible guilt to matchless glory.

At San Francisco's Fisherman's Wharf there is a Wax Museum where you can see scenes from various historic moments and the wax figures of renowned characters in our national and world history. That kind of thing appeals to me. It helps me to grasp more clearly what historical incidents were actually like. This is what we have in these three chapters of Romans. It is a demonstration—in terms of people—of how God works in human history, how he redeems and saves.

A Sad and Sober Story

The apostle has already declared that man is actually helpless to save himself. We have power to choose, we are expected to choose, and we are free to choose; but nevertheless, as Paul has made clear, God's will is worked out behind it all. We do not understand that, and so Paul turns the spotlight on Israel to demonstrate just how God works.

The story of Israel is sad and rather sobering. Here is a nation that thought of itself as having an inside track with God. Israel was the people of God, the chosen nation, close to God, with various advantages enjoyed by no other nation. Yet Paul begins this section with a clear acknowledgment that this nation is far, far away from God. Despite the possibilities they might have enjoyed, nevertheless, they are a long way from him. Paul does not express anger at that fact, nor does he come on with accusations. He begins with a description of the personal anguish this causes him:

> I speak the truth in Christ—I am not lying, my conscience confirms it in the Holy Spirit—I have great sorrow and unceasing anguish in my heart. For I could wish that I myself were cursed and cut off from Christ for the sake of my brothers, those of my own race, the people of Israel (vv. 1–4).

I am sure that to the Jews of his own day the apostle sounded like an enemy. As he preached and taught the riches that are in Christ Jesus and focused everything on the Person of Messiah, he became, in the eyes of the Jews, an enemy. This has remained true of the nation of Israel till today. They see Paul in that way. If a Jew reads the letter to the Romans, he probably would regard it as a gigantic put-down to the whole nation. Paul's ministry everywhere stirred up the antagonism of the Jews.

And yet Paul is not their enemy, as he himself makes it clear here. He is their loving, hurting friend. It breaks his heart that he has to say these things. The hurt is real. Paul tells us that these are not crocodile tears he is shedding. This is no phony protest, like some people who say, "I'm only telling you this because I love you," and then proceed to cut you to pieces. "No," Paul says, "my conscience supports me in this, and the Holy Spirit himself confirms that my anguish is genuine and real. It is deep and lasting." He describes it as "great sorrow and unceasing anguish."

To Trade Places in Hell

If you are grieving over someone you love, the trend of whose life is away from Christ and the things of God, you know how that anguish is always there beneath the surface of your heart. You may be enjoying yourself outwardly, and you may be at peace in many ways, but it is there, like a deep knot. The moment your thoughts go back to it you feel that unceasing anguish of heart. I don't think there is anything more devastating and more deeply felt than the love and concern of someone who sees another drifting into hurt, destruction, danger, despair, and perhaps even death, and who feels helpless to do anything about it. That was the apostle's position. His anguish was so deep he declares that if it were possible (fortunately it isn't) he would be willing to take their place in hell, if only they could find Christ! That kind of commitment is rare in humanity.

In Exodus 32, we find Moses saying something very similar. He came down from the mountain and found the people dancing around the golden calf, conducting themselves in riotous ways, and he intervened with God on their behalf. "Lord, if it be possible, blot this sin from their lives," he said. "But if not, blot me out of your book." That touches me. I confess that I have loved ones for whom I would be willing, gladly, to die that they might be in glory. I would be glad to give up the rest of my earthly life. But I can't think of anyone for whom I would be willing to give up my hope for eternity. And yet that is what the apostle is feeling. He knows it isn't possible, but he says, "If I could, I would."

What a lesson this is on how to approach someone you want to help, someone who isn't very eager to receive what you have to say. You never come on—Paul never does—with accusations, or with bitter words or denunciations or even with the issues that separate you.

Perhaps you have heard of the man who said to a friend, "I hear you dismissed your pastor. What was wrong?" The friend said, "Well, he kept telling us we were going to hell." The man said, "What does the new pastor say?" The friend said, "The new pastor keeps saying we're going to hell, too." "So what's the difference?" "Well," the friend said, "the difference is that when the first one said it, he sounded like he was glad of it; but when the new man says it, he sounds like it is breaking his heart." That is what Paul is saying here. It is breaking his heart as he has to tell the Romans these things.

Part of the reason for this anguish is made clear in what Paul says next. Paul recognizes the tremendous possibilities that the Jews had, of which they failed to take any advantage.

> Theirs is the adoption as sons; theirs the divine glory, the covenants, the receiving of the law, the temple worship and the promises. Theirs are the patriarchs, and from them is traced the human ancestry of Christ, who is God over all, forever praised! Amen (vv. 4,5).

I am reminded of a young man with whom I shared a ministry a number of years ago in Southern California. He had a brilliant mind, a powerful personality, keen insights into the

Scriptures, great effectiveness in what he said, and he was a convincing speaker. He is now a broken man, having drifted from the faith—an alcoholic, perhaps dying. What sorrow that brought to my heart when I heard of it, as I thought of the great possibilities he had that are now being wasted. This is the way the apostle feels about the nation of Israel. Look at these advantages—eight of them are listed.

First, they were chosen as the people of God. There is no doubt about that. God makes it very clear that he separated this nation—the descendants of Abraham through the twelve sons of Jacob and the tribes that came from them—as his people. He called them that: "Behold, Israel is my son." He dealt with them as the specially chosen people of God. Gentiles have not always understood that, and many times I think they resent it. Someone has put it:

> "How odd
> Of God,
> To choose
> The Jews!"

But God really did choose them. Their position was different than any other nation of their day, and Paul acknowledges it.

Second, to the Jews was given the divine glory. By that Paul means the Shekinah, the bright cloud that followed Israel through the wilderness and later abode in the holy of holies in the tabernacle marking the presence of God himself among his people. Centuries later, when the temple was built by King Solomon, the cloud of glory again came and filled the holy of holies, and the people knew that God had recognized his ties with this remarkable people and was living among them. To them belonged the glory.

Third, the Jews also had the covenants, Paul points out, those remarkable agreements that God made with Abraham, Isaac, and Jacob, with Moses and David, in which God committed himself to do things for that nation that he has never broken. God took the initiative to make these covenants with this strange and wonderful people.

Fourth, Paul says, the Jews had the law. This was their dearest and greatest treasure, and it still is. I recently finished reading the book *In the Beginning* by the contemporary Jewish writer, Chaim Potok, in which he describes how the Jews love the Torah, the scrolls of the Law. They have a service set aside in which the men of the congregation take the scrolls of the law and dance with them. Potok records how one of the young lads says to himself, "I wonder if the Goyim (Gentiles) ever feel this way about the Word of God," Yes, the law was their greatest treasure.

Fifth, Paul argues, the Jews had the temple worship. Not only did they have the law, but God had carefully and meticulously described how the people should conduct themselves. He told them the kinds of offerings to bring, the ritual to carry out, and he designed beautiful ways of reminding them of the truth that he had taught them through direct revelation. The Jews had the temple itself, one of the most beautiful buildings ever built by men. It was the glory of Israel, and it was still there in our Lord's day, and while Paul was writing this letter.

Sixth, the Jews had the promises. Those are still to be found in the pages of the Old Testament—promises of a time when the Jews would lead the nations of the world. From the Jews would come a universal reign, a world King, and Jerusalem would be the center of the earth. Government would flow from the city of Jerusalem throughout the whole earth. Those promises are still there, and God means to fulfill them.

Seventh, Paul says, the Jews had the patriarchs, those tremendous men whose names are household words all over the world—Abraham, Moses, David, and others. We think we are blessed in having leaders like Washington, Jefferson, and Lincoln, but even they are not as widely known as these great names from Israel.

Finally (*eighth*), the supreme blessing was that Jesus himself, the Messiah, came from Israel. From the Jews is traced the human ancestry of Christ. Notice Paul does not say that Christ belonged to Israel—he came from them. He belongs to the world because, as the apostle adds, "He is God over all, to be praised forever!" This is one of the clearest and most definite statements of the deity of Jesus that comes from the apostle's pen. I know there are manuscripts suggesting that this is to be translated as a closing doxology: "God be blessed and praised forever." But the best manuscripts do not put it that way at all. The most ancient texts agree that the apostle wrote, "Christ is God over all, blessed and praised forever!"

Approaching Crisis

And yet, with all these fantastic advantages, with the remarkable achievements and possibilities of this nation, the Jews of Paul's day were violently anti-Christian. They could not stand the idea that Jesus was their Messiah. Paul could see evidence, even at this early date, of the approaching crisis between the Jews and the Romans that would result in the destruction of the city of Jerusalem and judgment upon this nation. They would be scattered throughout the nations of the world for centuries.

This letter was written about 62 A.D., and already events were moving to bring about that final confrontation in 70 A.D. when the Roman armies would surround the city and eventually break through the walls, destroy the temple, level it to the ground, and take the Jews captive or drive them out into all the nations of the world, fulfilling the word of Jesus.

Now Paul raises a question, and here he gets into the heart of this chapter: Since Israel has proved to be faithless, does this mean that God was also faithless? Has God failed? Did Israel's failure come about because God is not able to save those whom he wants to save? Many people still think this is the problem. They wonder if God is really able to save someone he calls, so this question is relevant in our day.

Paul answers by launching upon a great statement that sets forth the faithfulness of God—but in terms that we struggle with. I want to warn you before we get started that you are going to have a difficult time with the ninth chapter of Romans. Way back in the prophet Isaiah's day, God had said to Isaiah, "For my thoughts are not your thoughts, neither are your ways my ways. . . . For as the heavens are higher than the earth, so are my ways higher than your ways, and my thoughts than your thoughts" (Isa. 55:8,9 RSV). Whatever else those words might mean, they certainly imply that there are times when God is going to act in ways we don't understand, ways that seem to us absolutely contrary to the way he should act.

Surely this is one of the major problems we face in dealing with God. There have been times when I have been bewildered and baffled by God's behavior. I have seen solutions to certain problems; I could see how to work them out —but God seemed totally unable to catch on. Even when I told him how to solve a situation, rather than take the simple steps (as I saw them) that would have worked out the solutions, he persisted in going into deeply involved relationships and circumstances that seemed to have no bearing at all on the working out of that problem. I am confronted, finally, with the truth of Isaiah's words. God is beyond me. Now, that is the attitude we must keep in mind as we go through this chapter.

No Natural Advantages

Paul introduces this to us by showing us some of the principles by which God carries out his great work. The first one is this: the fact that God may grant great opportunities and special privileges to people is no certain indication that God guarantees to save those people. Here is how Paul establishes his argument. First, he says, salvation is never based on natural advantages:

> It is not as though God's word had failed. For not all who are descended from Israel are Israel. Nor because they are his descendants are they all Abraham's children (vv. 6,7).

Two of the patriarchs are mentioned, Abraham and Jacob, for Israel, of course, is another name for Jacob. God named

Jacob Israel after he wrestled with the angel, for Israel means "A prevailer with God." God made Jacob, the usurper, into a conqueror. But those who are his descendants are not necessarily involved in all those promises. Even those who are physical descendants of Abraham, the greatest of the patriarchs, are not all included in the salvation promise of God.

Therefore, we can draw the conclusion that salvation is never based on natural advantages. It is not inherited. Your family may be Christians but that does not make you a Christian. You may have great opportunities for Bible study and obtaining Bible knowledge, and maybe you have taken advantage of them—but that does not necessarily make you a Christian. These special privileges that come to us by natural means are never the basis for God's redemption. That is the first thing we have to understand. Ancestry does not guarantee redemption.

Rather, Paul says, God's salvation is always based on a divine promise:

> On the contrary, "Through Isaac shall your offspring come." In other words, it is not the natural children who are God's children, but it is the children of promise who are regarded as Abraham's offspring. For this was how the promise was stated: "At the appointed time I [God] will return, and Sarah shall have a son" (vv. 7–9).

This takes us back to the eighteenth chapter of Genesis, where God said in effect to Abraham and Sarah, "I will come back, and Sarah, whose womb has been barren all her life—who has never had a child, who is now ninety years of age and, from a natural point of view, couldn't possibly have a child—is going to have a baby." It was a biological miracle, and that was God's promise. It involved his own supernatural activity. His promise is based on what he does, not upon what men do.

As you well know, Ishmael was Abraham's oldest son. He was thirteen years older than Isaac. By rights, as the firstborn son, he should have inherited the promises God made to Abraham. But instead, Isaac inherited those promises. Ishmael stands as a symbol of the futility of expecting God to honor our ideas of how he is to act. Do you remember how Ishmael was born? Sarah said to Abraham one day, "Do you expect God to do everything? He has promised you a son, but you are getting old. Time's wasting. Surely, God doesn't expect you to leave it all up to him!" So she suggested that he take her Egyptian servant. He did, and she conceived and bore a son. Abraham brought Ishmael before God and said, "God, here is my son. Will you fulfill your promises to him?" God said, "No, I won't. That is not the one. He must come by divine promise."

Find the Promise

This is an important principle in Scripture. I meet many people who get an idea of what they think God ought to do. They misread the promises about prayer, for instance, and think that if they pray for what they want, God has to do it. But what this teaches us very plainly is that God is committed to do only what he has promised to do. If you want God to act on your behalf, find a promise that he has given.

The many "faith healers" have taught over the years that God has promised he would heal all physical ailments. They tell people to claim healing from God. If we would just claim what God has promised, they say God will do it. I have been studying the Scriptures for thirty years or more, and I can't find that promise! God has never, anywhere, promised to heal all physical illnesses. He does heal, and often he will heal in response to the requests of his children —but he has never *promised* that he will. Therefore, we are wrong when we try to claim from God something that he never promised to do. That is why anything expected from God must rest upon a promise that he has already given. Otherwise it is wholly his grace that supplies an answer to our requests. That is the second principle here.

Now we come to the third, which is even more difficult to handle:

Not only that, but Rebecca's children had one and the same father, our ancestor Isaac. Yet, before the twins were born or had done anything good or bad—in order that God's purpose in election might stand: not by works but by him who calls— she was told, "The older will serve the younger" (vv. 10–12).

Do you remember who Rebecca was? She was Isaac's wife. He found her through Abraham's servant, who had been sent to find God's choice for him. When their twin sons were born God told Rebecca that the elder should serve the younger. That is a remarkable statement, and Paul confirms it with a quotation from Malachi 1:2,3:

Just as it is written, "Jacob I loved, but Esau I hated."

Many have struggled over those words. But all the apostle is saying is that it is clear from this story that, first, ancestry does not make any difference (these boys had the same father), and, second, what they will do in their lives—including the choices they will make—ultimately will not make any difference. Before they were able to make choices —either good or bad—God had said to their mother, "The elder shall serve the younger." By that he implied not only that there would be a difference in the nations that followed (the descendants of these two men) and that one would be in the place of honor and the other would not, but also that the personal destinies of these two men were involved as well. I think that is clear from the record of history. Jacob forever stands for the faith that God honors and wants men to have. Jacob was a scheming, rather weak character—not very lovable. Esau, on the other hand, was a rugged individualist—much more admirable, when he was growing up, than Jacob. But through the course of their lives, Jacob was the one who was brought to faith, and Esau was not.

I remember hearing of a man who said to a noted Bible teacher, "I'm having trouble with this verse, 'Jacob have I loved, but Esau have I hated.' How could God ever say 'Esau have I hated'?" The Bible teacher said, "I have trouble with that verse, too, but my problem is not quite the same.

I have no trouble in understanding the words 'Esau have I
hated.' What bothers me is how God could ever say 'Jacob
have I loved'!" Read the life of Jacob and you will see why.

To Love Less

Now, I do admit that we must not read this word "hated"
as though God actually disliked Esau and would have nothing to do with him and treated him with contempt. That is
what we often mean when we say we hate someone. Jesus
used this same word when he said, "If anyone comes to me
and does not hate his father and mother, his wife and children, his brothers and sisters—yes, even his own life—he
cannot be my disciple" (Luke 14:26). Clearly he is not saying that we have to treat our mothers and fathers and wives
and children and our own lives with contempt and disre-
spect. He just means that *he* is to have preeminence over all
else. Hatred, in that sense, means to love less. We are to love
these less than we love him.

God did not hate Esau, in any absolute sense. In fact he
blessed him. He made of him a great nation. He gave him
promises which he fulfilled to the letter. What these verses
imply is that God set his heart on Jacob, to bring him to
redemption, and all Jacob's followers would reflect the possibilities of that. As Paul has argued already, they were not
all necessarily saved by that heritage, but Jacob would forever stand for what God wants men to be, and Esau would
forever stand as a symbol of what he does not like.

Do you know where the final confrontation of Jacob and
Esau is recorded in the Scriptures? It was when Jesus stood
before Herod the king. Herod was an Idumean, an Edomite,
a descendant of Esau. Jesus was, through David, a descendant of Jacob. There, standing face-to-face, were Jacob and
Esau! Herod has nothing but contempt for the King of the
Jews, and Jesus will not open his mouth in the presence of
Herod. This is God's strange and mysterious way of dealing
with humanity.

Paul is teaching us here that God has a sovereign, elective

principle which he carries out on his terms. Here are those terms: Salvation is never based on natural advantages. Never! What you are by nature does not enter into the picture of whether you are going to be redeemed or not.

Second, salvation is always based on a promise that God gives. That is why we are exhorted in the Scriptures to believe the promises of God. In some mysterious way, it includes our necessity to be confronted with those promises, and to give a willing and voluntary submission to them. I do not understand that, but Paul brings it up a little later in this chapter when he discusses the harmony, as far as we can understand it, between the free will of men and the sovereign choice of God.

The third principle is that salvation never takes any notice of whether we are good or bad. Never! That is what was established here. In behavior these children were neither good nor bad, yet God chose Jacob and passed over Esau. Since, in God's sight, all children are born part of a lost race, what difference could moral or immoral behavior make?

Now I want to ask you this question: How do you react to what we have covered so far? Is there something in you that wants to cry out to God and say, "God, that's unfair! That isn't right!"? Then relax, because you are normal. There is something in us, called the flesh, that reacts to this; it doesn't like it. Paul picks that up later in this chapter and we will face it squarely and find out what we can about this sense of God's apparent unfairness. But in the meantime, let us reverently accept the fact that God is greater than we are. He knows more than we, he knows what he is doing, and everything he does will always be consistent with his character. God is love. Whether we can understand it or not, that is where it is going to come out.

2

Let God Be God

There was a time when almost everyone on earth believed the earth was flat. At the time it was a very comfortable theory to live with; it was safe, easy to understand. Now, believing this theory did not make it true, but it was easier to handle and it made life more predictable. In reading accounts of the time, we learn that people became rather upset when they encountered some evidence that this was not true. As more and more scientists began to say that the earth was really round and not flat, contrary to the way it looked to their eyes, and that it was spinning on its axis and floating in a great sea of space, people grew very upset.

Religious people, especially, were disturbed, for they believed with all their heart that the Bible taught that the earth was flat. In fact, they would quote certain passages that seemed to indicate this. So there was a great deal of controversy over the issue. It was a long time before people began to realize that the new evidence really made God appear more wonderful and more powerful than he ever had before. People also began to discover that there were certain verses and passages, overlooked before, which supported this new evidence. They could see how biblical revelation could be fitted within the context of this new truth.

I think that is also our problem when it comes to a passage like Romans 9. Many of us have grown up thinking that God is flat, that he is rather safe and easy to understand, and that he fits very comfortably into the pattern we have made for him. He is predictable, and we find ourselves secure with these little theological boxes into which we have crammed God.

We have already learned that it is very easy for us to misread God's actions. We look at history, we look at what is happening in contemporary events, we look at what the Bible itself records about God's actions, and it is easy for us to misread these and to think that God intends to do something that he really does not. God operates in line with certain principles—*his* principles—three of which have already been set forth in this chapter.

The Right to Choose

God does not grant salvation on the basis of the privileges he may have bestowed, nor does he redeem apart from his promise to do so, nor on the basis of any human works. Well then, what is the basis on which God chooses? Paul's answer, which we take up now in the second half of Romans 9, is that God's choice is based upon his sovereign right to choose. God has a right to choose whom he will. That is the final resolution of the problem:

> What then shall we say? Is God unjust? Not at all! For he says to Moses,
> > "I will have mercy on whom I have mercy,
> > and I will have compassion on whom I have
> > compassion."
> It does not, therefore, depend on man's desire or effort, but on God's mercy. For the Scripture says to Pharaoh: "I raised you up for this very purpose, that I might display my power in you and that my name might be proclaimed in all the earth." Therefore God has mercy on whom he wants to have mercy, and he hardens whom he wants to harden (vv. 14–18).

You may not like it, but what this says is that the ultimate reason for God's choice of anyone is that God chose him. He chooses whom he wants.

I think this is the truth about God which men dislike the most. God is a sovereign being. He is not responsible—nor answerable—to anyone. He is totally, absolutely sovereign. We don't like that, because to us sovereignty is always connected with tyranny. To trust anyone with that kind of power is to put ourselves in the hands of someone who might destroy us, and we instinctively fight that. We fight it in our national life, in our family life, and in our individual relationships. We do not trust anyone with absolute power over us. The Constitution of the United States is based on that concept. No one can be trusted with absolute power. We have checks and balances built into our government. We divide it into three parts, and pit one division against the other, so that they all watch each other. We do not believe that even the best of men can be trusted with absolute power.

It is no wonder, therefore, that when we come to the Scriptures and confront the fact that God has absolute power, we become uneasy and troubled. But if God had to give an answer to anyone, that being or person to whom God had to account would really be God. The very idea of God is that he is sovereign. He does what he pleases, what he wants to do. What we must do is get rid of the idea that his sovereignty is going to be destructive to us. It is not, at all. As we will see before this is over, his sovereignty is our only hope!

Paul says here that God declares his own sovereignty. God said to Moses, "I will have mercy on whom I have mercy, and I will have compassion on whom I have compassion." Now, Moses was a great example of God's way of choosing someone to bless. Who was Moses that God should choose him? Moses was no one in himself. In fact, he was a murderer. On one occasion, in a fit of temper, he killed a man. Then, instead of turning himself in for justice, he hid the body in the sand. He was a criminal and a fugitive from justice. For forty years he had been living in the desert, a nobody. No one had heard of him. But the Lord picked him up and made him a messenger of God and gave him a name that became known throughout history. He set him in authority over the greatest kingdom the world had ever known at that time and used him in a most remarkable way. Why? God chose to do so. He had the right to do that.

On the other hand, God also demonstrated his sovereignty with Pharaoh. He took a man who was no better than Moses (in fact, Scripture tells us God often places the basest of men in power) and put him on a throne and gave him authority over all the nation of Egypt. Then, when Moses confronted him, God allowed Pharaoh to continue to resist God's will. God could have kept him from resisting, but he didn't. He allowed him to do what *all* men do by nature—resist God. So Pharaoh held out against God in order, as this verse says, that God might demonstrate his power and attract the attention of men everywhere to his greatness.

That bothers us. We think anyone who boasts about his greatness, who tries constantly to get people to notice how great he is, is a braggart and conceited. We don't like such people—largely because we are jealous of them! We want to be the one standing up there getting people to admire our greatness.

But, you see, God must do this for the welfare of his creatures. In our consistent tendency to think of God as nothing but an enlarged man, we attribute to God our own motives. When man seeks his own glory, he is destructive. He must necessarily put others down to elevate himself. But what God does is necessary to the welfare and benefit of his creatures. The more his creatures understand the goodness and greatness and glory of God, the richer their lives will be, and the more they will enjoy life. Jesus said, "This is eternal life, that they might know thee, the only true God, and Jesus Christ, whom thou hast sent." So when God invites men to consider his glory and seeks to stimulate men to think about his greatness, it is not because God's ego needs to be massaged—it is because God's creatures require this for their best welfare. Therefore, God finds ways to do it, even using men to resist his will, so that there might be an occasion to display his greatness and power.

All the Bitter Charges

Paul's conclusion, therefore, is that God has mercy on whom he wants to have mercy, and he hardens whom he wants to harden. Immediately someone objects. We all feel this objection, I am sure. We object in the same words as verse 19:

> One of you will say to me: "Then why does God still blame us? For who can resist his will?"

In that brief statement are hidden all the accusations and bitter charges that men bring against God: God is the one responsible for all human evil! It isn't us; it is God ultimately who is to blame! This accusation appears in many different forms in human history. What does man do with this essential truth about God's nature, his sovereignty? He uses it to blame God for all evil.

Verses 20 through 29 give us Paul's answer to this, and we will look at that in due time. But right now I want to spend a moment with this charge that men bring against God. What it is really saying is, "All right, Paul. You say that God uses men for whatever he wants to use them for. Men cannot resist him. Pharaoh could not resist God's use of him. God used him to oppose what he sent Moses to do in Egypt. Pharaoh was merely an instrument in God's hands. So God uses men to do evil, then he turns around and blames them for the evil and punishes them for doing what he made them do! That's not just, that's not fair! God himself must agree that it is not fair to make someone do something, and then punish him for doing it. The very sense of justice, which God himself gave us, is offended by that!"

That sounds logical, doesn't it? How do you answer logic like that? Paul has four things to say in reply, and the first one is found in verse 20. Basically what he says here is, "All right, you man, whoever you are, you are charging God with injustice. You say he is not fair because he does this! Let's examine your credentials."

Who are you, O man, to talk back to God? "Shall what is formed say to him who formed it, 'Why did you make me like this?' "

"Let's take a look at this," Paul says. "Let's compare and consider the difference between man and God. Here is man, finite (that means his knowledge and understanding is limited) and frail. He has limited strength. He only lasts a little while—a breath of air and he is gone. The record shows us through the whole course of man's history that not only is man finite and frail, but, despite all his logic, time and time again man demonstrates how foolish he is. He makes atrocious blunders, even when he thinks he is doing the right thing. With all this array of logic and reason, he ends up making the most idiotic mistakes. Now, that kind of man is daring to stand up against the God who is mighty and wise, absolute in power and majesty, infinite in knowledge, knowing all things from beginning to end—not only all the things that are, but also all the things that could be. This puny pipsqueak of a man is daring to stand up and challenge the justice of a God like that!"

What Paul is saying is that even our logic is often wrong, because there are mysteries we do not reckon on, objectives we cannot discern, resistance about which we know nothing. So who are you, man, to stand and question the rightness of God? That is a good argument, isn't it? Are we equipped to challenge God in this way?

Look Who's Asking!

Perhaps the most helpful book in the Bible on this score is the Book of Job. Job was not a cavalier; he was not a skeptic, an atheist arguing against God. He was a devout man who loved God deeply. Yet he was a deeply puzzled and bewildered man who could not understand what God was doing with him. You know the story. Job was afflicted with a series of terrible boils and physical afflictions, and his family and all his wealth disappeared in a trip-hammer series of terrible catastrophes.

To top it all, he was afflicted by three torturers, who called themselves his friends. These men came to argue with him in his pain and despair, using the presupposition that all suffering must be caused by sin. Therefore Job's suffering meant that he somehow was a deep-dyed sinner, and all his pain was a result of refusing to let people know the terrible evil he must have done. They hounded poor Job, examined every crack and cranny of this argument, and plumbed it to its depths. Finally, in despair, Job cried out. He did not blame God—that is the glory of this book—he never once blamed God. He just said, "Lord, I don't understand it! Oh, if I could just come and stand before you and plead my case, I could show you how unfair it seems to me!"

So, in chapters 38 through 41, God appears before Job and says, "All right, Job, you wanted a chance to argue. You wanted to ask me some questions—here I am. But before you begin, I have some to ask you, to see if you are qualified to investigate me. Here are my questions: Where were you when I laid the foundation of the earth? Where were you when the morning stars sang together, and I flung the heavens into space? Were you there? Can you enter into the secrets of the sea? Do you understand how the rain works, and how the lightning appears? Do you understand these things, Job? Why, these are simple to me. How are you doing on them?"

Job has to hang his head. God goes on: "Look at the stars, Job. Can you order their courses? Can you make the Pleiades shine forth in the springtime? Can you make Orion stride across the winter sky, always on time? Can you handle the universe, Job?" And Job says, "No, I'm sorry; I don't qualify." God says, "All right, let me ask you some more questions."

Then, in a tremendous section that is really the key to the Book of Job, God uses the figures of Behemoth and Leviathan, two strange and formidable creatures, to examine Job's qualifications to handle satanic power. "Can you handle Satan? Do you know how to control this fantastic dragon who can wreck a third of the universe with his tail? Are you able to take him on?" Finally Job ends up on his face in the dust before God and says, "Lord God, I didn't know what I was getting into! I just meant to say a few things to you, but I am not in your league at all! I repent in sackcloth and ashes; I put my hand on my mouth. I have nothing to say to a God like you." That is Paul's argument here: "Who are you, O man, to reply against God? You don't understand even a tiny fraction of the things to be known, so how can you argue with such a God?"

Delegated Sovereignty

Paul's second argument follows. Even among men, he says, we exercise a form of sovereignty, and do we not have the right to do so?

> Does not the potter have the right to make out of the same lump of clay some pottery for noble purposes and some for common use? (v. 21)

Nobody questions that, do they? Doesn't a potter have the right to take the lump of clay that he is working with and divide it in half and make of one half a beautiful vase for the living room and out of the other a slop jar? Why yes, he has that right. No one tells the potter what he should do with his clay. Men exercise sovereignty like that and nobody questions it at all.

Well, at this point many people say, "But we're not clay! It's all right to do that with unfeeling clay, but human beings are not clay. We're people. We have feelings, sensitivities, and wills. Your analogy doesn't hold!" Well, you can extend the analogy to things that have feelings. What about the ways we treat plants and animals? Doesn't a gardener have the right to move plants around wherever he pleases? Just last week I tore out some plants and threw them away —good, healthy plants. Did I have the right to do that? Should my neighbors swear out a warrant for my arrest because I didn't ask permission of the plants first? Does a farmer have the right to send cattle to slaughter, to pick out certain ones that he thinks are nice and fat and slaughter them, while he keeps others a while longer? Do we ever challenge that? No. Men have that kind of authority—a kind of delegated sovereignty. Therefore, can we deny it to the one being who, in all the created universe, has the right, above all else? That is Paul's argument. It is hard to answer that, isn't it?

"But," someone says, "it still doesn't solve this problem of justice. It seems unfair." Paul's third argument says, "Then let us consider two possible motives in God's actions":

> What if God, choosing to show his wrath and make his power known, bore with great patience the objects of his wrath—prepared for destruction? What if he did this to make the riches of his glory known to the objects of his mercy, whom he prepared in advance for glory—even us, whom he also called, not only from the Jews but also from the Gentiles? As he says in Hosea:
>> "I will call them 'my people' who are not my people;
>> and I will call her 'my loved one' who is not my
>>   loved one,"
> and
>> "It will happen that in the very place where it
>>   was said to them,
>>   'You are not my people,' [Those are the Gentiles—us.]
>>   they will be called 'sons of the living God.'"
> Isaiah cries out concerning Israel: "Though the number of the Israelites should be like the sand by the sea, only the remnant will be saved. For the Lord will carry out his sentence on earth with speed and finality" (vv. 22–28).

What Paul is saying in this passage is that God may have purposes and objectives we do not see. But doesn't he have the right to those purposes? What if one of those objectives is not only to display his power and his wrath by allowing man to oppose him until he ultimately judges them, but also to display his amazing patience and longsuffering this way? Did you ever think about that? Did you ever think of how, for centuries and centuries, God has put up with the snarling, nasty, blasphemous, accusing remarks of men, and has done nothing to them? He has listened to all the cheap, shoddy, vulgar things men say about him, and has allowed them to treat him with hostility and anger, never doing a thing, but patiently enduring it. Paul says, "What if God does all that? What if it takes that kind of display of both the wrath of God and the patience of God to bring those of us whom he chooses to himself?" Something has to appear to us that makes us understand God. We are not forced to come to him; we are drawn to him. Therefore we have to respond, and something must make us respond. Is it not the wrath of God (which reveals his power) and the patience of God (which reveals his love) that draws us on?

All this, then, is necessary to bring some to glory. In other words, for some to be saved, some must be lost. I admit that is an inscrutable mystery. I don't understand it, but I don't have to. That's the whole thing. I cannot understand it at this point. There are factors in it which God cannot reveal. He will some day, but he doesn't now—not because he does not want to, but because I can't handle it. And neither can you. We have to accept it, nevertheless. Paul suggests here that without the display of wrath on God's part, no Gentiles ever would have been saved—only the elect of Israel, and only a remnant of them. But as it is, the Gentiles, those of us who never had the advantages that Israel had, are included, as Hosea and Isaiah both predicted.

Now the final and clinching argument, the fourth one, is found in verse 29:

> It is just as Isaiah said previously:
> > "Unless the Lord All-powerful had left us
> > descendants,
> > we would have become like Sodom,
> > and we would have been like Gomorrah."

I don't think there is a more desolate place on the face of the earth than the sites of Sodom and Gomorrah—just dreary, dry desert beside a briny sea in which nothing will live and around which nothing will grow. It is the most terrible place of desolation on the face of the earth! What

Paul argues here is that if God had not chosen to draw us to himself by an elective decree—something that makes men wake up and stop resisting him and start listening to him— none of us would ever be saved.

Born Lost

Clearly, we start thinking on this from the wrong premise. We start by thinking that everyone is in neutral, and unless they have an opportunity to be saved, they remain in neutral until it is too late for them to have a chance. But that isn't it at all! The truth is, we were born lost. We are already lost; we were lost in Adam. Adam lost the race, not we; but we are victims of his sin. There isn't a chance that any of us will do anything but resist God. Paul has said in chapter 3, "There is none that does good, no, not one! There is none that seeks after God, not one!" So you see, God is not shutting us away without a chance. His grace reaches out to us. Without it, no one would ever be saved at all. The whole race would be lost. God's justice would allow the race to be lost, but God's mercy reaches out to save many among us. That properly is his sovereign choice and that is where we must leave it.

The passage closes with a remarkable paragraph. At this point people ask, "How can we tell whether someone is chosen or not? If you can't tell by the advantages they have, how can you tell?" Here is the answer:

> What then shall we say? That the Gentiles, who did not pursue righteousness, have obtained it, a righteousness that is by faith; but Israel, who pursued a law of righteousness, has not attained it. Why not? Because they pursued it not by faith but as it were by works. They stumbled over the "stumbling stone." As it is written:
> "See, I lay in Zion a stone that causes men to
>   stumble
>   and a rock that makes them fall,
>   and the one who trusts in him will never be put to
>   shame" (vv. 30–33).

God says there is a way you can tell whether you are being drawn by the Spirit unto salvation or whether you are being permitted by God to remain where you already were, lost and condemned. The way you can tell is by what you do with Jesus. God has planted a stone in the midst of society. Now, when you walk down a path and come to a big flat rock in the middle of the path, there are two things you can do. You can stumble over it, or you can stand on it, one or the other. That is what God says Jesus is—a rock.

The Jews, who determined to work out their salvation on the basis of their own behavior, their own good works before God, stumbled over the stone. That is why the Jews rejected Jesus, and why many of them reject him to this day. They don't want to admit that they need a Savior, that they are not able to save themselves. No man is. But for those who see that they need a Savior, they have already been drawn by the Spirit of God, awakened by his grace, and made to understand what is going on in their lives. Therefore, their very desire to be saved, their awareness of their need for a Savior, causes them to accept Jesus. They stand upon that stone. Anyone who comes on that basis will never be put to shame.

Now that, God says, is the testing point. The crisis of humanity is Jesus. You can be very religious, you can spend hours and days or an entire lifetime following religious pursuits and apparently honoring God. But the test will always come: What do you do with Jesus? God put him in the midst of human society to reveal those whom he has called and those whom he has not. Jesus taught this very plainly: "No man can come to me unless the Father . . . draws him. . . . All that the Father gives me will come to me, and whoever comes to me I will never drive away" (John 6:44,37).

So what is left for us? To respond to Jesus, that is all. And to thank God that in doing so, we are not only doing what our hearts and consciences urge us to do, but we are responding in obedience to the drawing of the electing Spirit of God, who, in mercy, has chosen to bring us out of a lost humanity.

3

How to Be Saved

Brothers, my heart's desire and prayer to God for the Israelites is that they may be saved (Rom. 10:1).

I do not think there is any word in the Christian vocabulary that makes people more uncomfortable than the word "saved." People cringe when they hear it. Perhaps it conjures up visions of hot-eyed, zealous buttonholers—usually with bad breath—who walk up and grab you and say, "Brother, are you saved?" Or perhaps it raises visions of a tiny band of Christians at a street meeting in front of some saloon singing, "Give the winds a mighty voice, Jesus saves! Jesus saves!"

I will never forget the startled look on the face of a man who came up to me in a movie theater. The seat beside me was vacant, and he said, "Is this seat saved?" I said, "No, but I am." He promptly found a seat across the aisle. Somehow this word threatens all our religious complacency and angers the self-confident and the self-righteous alike.

And yet, when you turn to the Scriptures you find that this is an absolutely unavoidable word. Christians have to talk about men and women being saved because the fact is that men and women are lost. There is no escaping this fact:

The Bible clearly teaches that the human race into which we were born is already a lost race. This is why the good news of John 3:16 is that "God so loved the world that he gave his one and only Son, that whoever believes in him shall not perish—*not perish*—but have everlasting life." We can never deal realistically with life until we face up to this fundamental fact: People are not in the process of waiting until they die to be lost—they are already lost. It is the grace of God that reaches down and calls us out of that lostness and gives us an opportunity to come to Christ and be saved. Therefore "saved" is a perfectly legitimate word to use.

Paul is answering the question of why some who have little knowledge are saved while many who have much knowledge are not saved. Part of his answer was given in the ninth chapter, in which he explained that behind this strange mystery is the elective, sovereign choice of God. God chooses to call men to him—but not all men. But now he turns to the other side. Now we are confronted with the fact of human responsibility. It is true that God draws men to him; it is also true that no one will come unless he voluntarily responds to the appeal of God.

As we have seen, human knowledge is too limited to resolve this apparent conflict. But both sides are true. God calls men by an elective decree that is irresistible, and yet they must respond by a choice of their will, which they are free to make or not, as it pleases them. Let's see how Paul introduces this other side of the picture and brings before us Israel's responsibility:

> Brothers, my heart's desire and prayer to God for the Israelites is that they may be saved. For I can testify about them that they are zealous for God, but their zeal is not based on knowledge. Since they disregarded the righteousness that comes from God and sought to establish their own, they did not submit to God's righteousness (vv. 1–4).

Called through Our Prayers

Probably the most outstanding thing about this paragraph is this: despite Paul's profound conviction that God saves whomever he will by an irresistible choice, nevertheless this does not stop Paul from praying and yearning over his kinsmen according to the flesh, the nation of Israel. Clearly, prayer is not inconsistent with God's call. It is never right for us to say, "If God calls, there is nothing for us to do," because the way God calls is through the preaching of the Word and the praying of Christians, the yearning of their hearts over those who are not yet saved. Therefore, this is all part of God's program, and we need to see the importance that such prayer has in reaching people. Paul prayed for men. He writes in 1 Timothy 2:1–4,8:

> I urge, then, first of all, that requests, prayers, intercession and thanksgiving be made for everyone—for kings and all those in authority, that we may live peaceful and quiet lives in all godliness and holiness. This is good, and pleases God our Savior, who wants all men to be saved and to come to a knowledge of the truth. . . . I want men everywhere to lift up holy hands in prayer, without anger or disputing.

Prayer is a great factor in that call. C. S. Lewis has said some very helpful things in this regard. Speaking of prayer, he says,

> When we are praying about the result, say, of a battle or a medical consultation, the thought will often cross our minds that, if we only knew it, the event is already decided one way or the other. I believe this to be no reason for ceasing our prayers. The event certainly has been decided. In a sense, it was decided before all the worlds. But one of the things taken into account in deciding it, and therefore one of the things that really causes it to happen, may be this very prayer that we are now offering. [He then adds] Thus, shocking as it may sound, I conclude that we can at noon become part causes of an event occurring at ten o'clock.

That is, even our prayers *after* an event affect the event. Now that is strange to us, but I think it is true. We are up against a great mystery in the matter of prayer. C. S. Lewis adds:

There is no question whether an event has happened because of your prayer. When the event you prayed for occurs, your prayer has always contributed to it. When the opposite event occurs, your prayer has never been ignored; it has been considered and refused for your ultimate good and the good of the whole universe.

Those are deep matters, but perhaps that will help us. At least it is clear that Paul does not hesitate to pray, even though he knows God chooses whom he will.

The second emphasis that Paul makes in this paragraph is the zeal of Israel. "I bear testimony that Israel is zealous for God." And indeed they are. Perhaps the most noteworthy difference between an orthodox Jew and the average Gentile is right there. Jews take God seriously. Any of you who have seen *Fiddler on the Roof* or have read the writings of Chaim Potok, or other contemporary Jewish authors, know how true this is. The Jewish way of life is built around God. God is the most important element in all their thinking. They sacrifice anything and everything to the centrality of God in their national and community life.

That is in stark contrast to the average Gentile. Gentiles have religious feelings—all men do. Gentiles think of God, but God is on the periphery of Gentile life. I think we all demonstrate this. We are more casual about God. He is not the center of life, as he is in Jewish thought and action.

Yet the thing that amazed Paul, and amazes us today, is that the casual Gentile, who is not necessarily looking for God, nevertheless often finds him. He discovers God suddenly intruding into his life when he didn't expect him. He finds peace and rest and joy even when he isn't looking for it. But the Jew, with all his zeal, with his consummate desire to discover and to know God, fails to find peace and forgiveness and is not reborn into joy and love.

To Establish Their Own

Paul tells us why this is so. The reason is that the Jews sought to establish their own righteousness, and therefore they missed the gift of God, which is the righteousness of Christ, obtained without works. Anyone, Jew or Gentile, who seeks to establish his own righteousness, will be in the same boat. The problem with the Jews was that they were constantly trying their best to obey the law of Moses. They were failing to do so, of course, but they were not willing to admit that they failed. Thus they kept hoping and seeking and believing that God would accept them, even though they did not truly obey the law.

Now, there are many people like that today, both Jew and Gentile. In fact, to show you how true it is that Jews still think this way, I would like to quote a paragraph from a letter. A boy I know, who came from a Jewish background, received this letter recently from a rabbi. The rabbi wrote because he was troubled about the boy's faith in Christ:

> The basic question about religion is how to elevate man, and bring him into closer relationship with God. [That is the rabbi's view of the purpose of religion. It is to elevate man, not to change him.] We believe that God revealed to us in the Torah [the law of Moses] how he wants us to live, so that we can be in harmony with his divine purpose. Our role and religious purpose is to obey God's laws—to love him and to obey him. We exercise our free will by proper intention and, *through having done the good deeds,* are elevated so that it becomes progressively easier and more natural to continue to do good and to resist evil.

That is the current Jewish view of how to be right before God—simply keep trying until it becomes easier and easier, and finally you stand righteous before God. Paul says this is the problem; anyone who seeks to come before God on that basis is doomed to failure. Such a person does not and cannot obey the law. Paul goes on to show us why they can't and to reveal to us that the issue is always Jesus.

> Christ is the end of the law so that there may be righteousness for everyone who believes (10:4).

Christ is the end of the law—any kind of law—so that there may be righteousness for everyone who believes. Of course this does not mean that Christ does away with law. He does away with law as far as its effect in bringing you to God is concerned. He makes a total end of it. And, as we have seen in this letter, the reason is clear. What was the purpose of law? Why, to make us aware that there is something wrong with us. If you don't have a standard to try to live up to, you have no idea that there is anything wrong with you. You think everything you do is natural, and therefore right. We hear this argument all the time: anything that is natural is right. This is because more and more today the law is being set aside.

Now, the law was given to make us realize there are things that feel natural but are wrong. These are destroying us. All the injury and death and darkness that come into our lives come because of the things we are doing and the attitudes we have. We are producing the problem. We think it comes from everyone else, but law helps us to see that we are wrong. But once it has shown us that then what good is it? It can do no more.

At that point, unless we come to Christ, there is no way out. The law cannot cure our evil; it can only show it to us. At that point the law becomes our schoolmaster to bring us to Christ, as Paul puts it in Galatians 3:24. This is the end of the law; this is its purpose. It has been fulfilled when it does that work and brings you to Jesus Christ. He can change you. He can give you new life. He can wipe out the old pattern of failures and all the hurt and agony and anguish you have been going through and give you a wholly new heart. Therefore Christ is the end of law, that there may be righteousness to everyone who believes in him.

In his logical way, Paul is very careful to show us how this works. He quotes Moses to prove what the law is for:

> Moses describes in this way the righteousness that is by the law: "The man who does these things [fulfills the law] will live by them" (10:5).

Moses said that in Leviticus: "Here is the law, the Ten Commandments. Anybody who does these things will live. That

is, God will bless him, fulfill his humanity, make him enjoy
all that God had for man in the beginning. It will all come
if a man will simply obey these ten rules." You know, when
you read the Ten Commandments, they always seem so
reasonable, they seem so easy to obey. This is the way people have always reacted to them. You say to yourself, "Why,
this is not difficult. I can do that easily. All I have to do is
just decide to do it, that's all!"

The Gospel According to Moses

But when you actually start to do it, you soon discover a
rebelliousness inside that sooner or later stops you from
doing what you want to do. We have seen this all through
Romans. So it ends up that the law reveals the evil in your
life. Moses said the law was given to make people try to live
this way. He said that he who did these things would live.

Now Paul goes on to quote Moses again. He doesn't say
that Moses said the next part, but he did, in the book of
Deuteronomy. Paul sets the faith-way to God right next to
the law-way:

> But the righteousness that is by faith says, "Do not say in your
> heart, 'Who will ascend into heaven?' " (that is, to bring Christ
> down), or " 'Who will descend into the deep?' " (that is, to
> bring Christ up from the dead), [The comments in parentheses
> are Paul's] But what does it say?
>   "The word is near you;
>   it is in your mouth and in your heart";
> that is, the word of faith that we are proclaiming: (vv. 6–8)

It may startle you to realize that Paul is saying here that
Moses taught salvation by grace through faith just as much
as Paul did. Moses knew that the law would not work. Why,
even as Moses was bringing the tablets down from the
mountaintop the people at the bottom of the mountain had
broken all ten of the commandments before the law was
given to them. And after they had received them they
promptly broke them again.

Moses knew that the people could not keep them, but Moses also taught that God had provided another way by which people could be delivered when they failed to keep the law. He saw clearly that God would lay the foundation for salvation in the incarnation, crucifixion, and resurrection of Jesus. That is why Paul quotes these words from Deuteronomy. Moses foresaw the coming of Christ from heaven, and he saw the resurrection, the raising of Jesus from the dead. Paul clearly indicates that all along God had this basis in mind as the way people were to come to Christ.

When the angels sang the song to the shepherds in the darkness of the night on the plains of Bethlehem, and the glory of the Lord broke out upon them out there in the fields, the angel of the Lord said to them, "Behold, I bring you good tidings of great joy, which shall be to all men; for unto you is born this day in the city of David a savior, who is Christ the Lord." This was the historic fulfillment of the way God had been actually saving people for centuries before this. Now it is being worked out in history—but God had been saving people who saw beyond the law to the work of Christ long before that.

And when the angels, in the brightness of the Easter sunrise, said to the woman at the tomb of Jesus, "Go and tell his disciples that he is risen, as he said," that was the culmination of God's program to work out human redemption quite apart from any effort on man's part. Jesus had done it all. That is why Paul points out here that Moses understood that the way to lay hold of and personally appropriate the value of these incredible events was to believe the divine announcement with the whole man, with the whole being. That is why he adds,

But what does it say?
    "The word is near you;
        It is in your mouth and in your heart";
    that is, the word of faith we are proclaiming:

The mouth symbolizes the outward man, the intellectual understanding of what has happened to him expressed in words; the heart is the inner man, the will, the spirit deep within us understanding the basis on which God saves. And lest anyone miss it, Paul goes on with these clear words:

> That if you confess with your mouth, "Jesus is Lord," and believe in your heart that God raised him from the dead, you will be saved. For it is with your heart that you believe and are justified, and it is with your mouth that you confess and are saved (v. 9).

That is the clearest statement in the Word of God on how to be saved. Paul makes it very simple. He says it begins with the confession of the mouth that "Jesus is Lord."

Right to Lordship

Paul does not mean you have to stand up in public somewhere and announce your belief that Jesus is Lord before you are saved, although this does not exclude that. He means that the mouth is the symbol of the conscious acknowledgment to ourselves of what we believe. It means we have come to the place where we recognize that Jesus has the right to lordship in our lives. Up to this point we have been lord of our lives. We have run our own affairs, feeling we have the right to make our own decisions according to what we want. But there comes a time, as God's Spirit works in us and we see the reality of life as God has made it to be, that we realize Jesus is Lord. He is Lord of our past, to forgive us our sins; he is Lord of our present, to dwell within us and to guide, direct, and control every area of our life; he is Lord of our future, to lead us into glory at last. Christ is Lord of life, Lord of death—he is Lord over all things.

As Jesus himself said after his resurrection, "All power is given unto me, in heaven and on earth"—*all* power. Jesus is in control of history; he is running all human events. He stands at the end of every path on which men go, and he is the ultimate One we all must reckon with. That is why Peter says in Acts 4:12, "Salvation is found in no one else; for there is no other name under heaven given to men by which we must be saved." You cannot read the Book of Acts without recognizing that the basic creed of the early Christians was "Jesus is Lord."

These are days when one hears much about mantras, words one is supposed to repeat when he meditates. I suggest we adopt this as a mantra: Jesus is Lord. Wherever you are, say it again and again, to remind yourself of this great truth. When Peter stood up to speak on the day of Pentecost, this was his theme, "Jesus is Lord." The thousands of Jews listening to him could not deny what he pointed out— that Jesus had lived a unique life, had been witnessed to by the prophets before him, had died a most remarkable death, had been raised from the dead in a most astonishing way, then had poured out supernatural signs from heaven, evidences they could not deny. They had to recognize the fact above all facts, that Jesus was Lord whether they liked it or not. Therefore, the great question of all time is, "What are you going to do with Jesus?"

Paul tells us here that Jesus is Lord, and if you have come to the place where you believe in your heart that he is risen and available and you are ready to say to yourself, "Jesus is *my* Lord," then God acts. At that moment God does something. No man can do it, but God can. He begins to bring about all that is wrapped up in this word "saved." Your sins will be forgiven: God imparts to you a standing of righteous worth in his sight; he loves you; he gives you the Holy Spirit to live within you; he makes you a son in his family; he gives you an inheritance for eternity; you are joined to the body of Christ as members of the family of God; you are given Jesus himself to live within you, to be your power over evil, over the world, the flesh, and the devil; and you will live life in an entirely different way than before. That is what happens when you confess with your mouth that Jesus is Lord and believe in your heart that God raised him from the dead.

He Becomes Savior

It is helpful to see that nowhere in all the Scriptures are men ever asked to believe in Jesus as Savior. They are asked to believe in him as Lord. When you believe in him as Lord, he becomes your Savior. But you don't accept Christ as a Savior—you accept him as Lord, as the one who is in charge of all things, including you. When you come to that point, when you respond with the whole man, then God says the work of redemption is done. The miracle occurs.

"Well," someone says, "what if I'm not elect? What if all the time I've been wanting God and seeking God, and then it turns out I'm not chosen?" Anyone who talks that way (and people do talk that way) is indicating he has never understood what Paul is saying here. For if you believe in Christ you have given proof that you are elect. As Jesus himself put it, "No man can come to me except my Father draw him." You can't believe in God until God has called you and drawn you. The very desire to believe is part of that drawing, therefore we needn't struggle over this apparent conflict.

What Scripture everywhere confronts us with is the necessity for every individual to settle the question, "Is Jesus Lord of your life? Is he your Lord? Have you enthroned him and acknowledged him where God has placed him, as king over all the earth, the Lord of glory, the one who is in charge of all things?" When you do, that is the moment when redemption begins to occur. Now, see how Paul confirms this in the verses that follow:

> As the Scripture says, "He who believes in him will not be put to shame." [Here Paul quotes Isaiah. It is not on the basis of works, but on the basis of belief—he who accepts what Christ does, who believes on him, will not be put to shame.] For there is no difference between Jew and Gentile—the same Lord is Lord of all and richly blesses all who call on him, for, "Everyone who calls on the name of the Lord will be saved." [That is the word of Joel the prophet.] (vv. 11–13)

These verses indicate that this is not something new with Paul, but it is something all the Scriptures have taught, both Old and New Testaments alike—that faith is the way by which we lay hold of what God has to give us. It is never gained by earning it or by trying to be good, or by the good outweighing the bad, but simply by acknowledging that Jesus Christ has done it all on our behalf, and opening our hearts to his lordly control.

John 1:11–12 tells us, "He came to that which was his own, and his own did not receive him. Yet to all who received him, to those who believed in his name, he gave the right to become children of God. . . ." So if you have asked him to come into your heart and received him as Lord, and you mean to allow him to be the controlling center of your life, I can tell you on the authority of the Word of God that you have been saved!

4

Have They Not Heard?

This section of Romans 10 brings before us the answer to one of the most frequently asked questions we hear, especially from non-Christians: "What happens to all the people who never hear about Jesus?" That question is phrased in a variety of forms, but basically it is the expressed concern of many—especially when they hear Christians talking about the uniqueness of Jesus, that he is the only way by which men can come to God.

In the first part of the chapter, the apostle said that in order for any individual person to be salvaged from the wreck of humanity, he must call upon the name of the Lord. Well, how do you do that? How do you call on the name of the Lord? Paul goes on in verse 14 to outline the steps that lie behind this essential to salvation—calling on the name of the Lord.

How, then, can they call on the one they have not believed in? And how can they believe in the one of whom they have not heard? And how can they hear without someone preaching to them? And how can they preach unless they are sent? As it is written, "How beautiful are the feet of those who bring good news!"

There are five steps involved in calling on the name of the Lord. Paul begins with that final step, the call itself. He traces it back for us so we can see what is involved in bringing people to the place where they cry out to God and are saved, born again, made alive in Jesus Christ. Paul begins by stressing the fact that each person individually must call on God. "*Everyone* who calls on the name of the Lord will be saved." There has to be an individual, personal conviction. It is not enough to come and sit under the preaching of the gospel. Some people think that if they go to church regularly and hear the gospel they will be saved. No, there has to be a time when you personally call on the name of the Lord.

Beyond Emotions

Behind the call is belief. Paul says, "How, then, can they call on the one they have not believed in?" So there has to be belief. That means the mind has to be engaged—the intellect is called into play. I think this is important because so many people feel it is enough for the emotions to be stirred. I have been in many evangelistic services where people were stirred emotionally, but did not understand anything about what God had done. They had nothing to believe in; they were just stirred up to want something.

Years ago there was a great evangelist named Gypsy Smith. Born a gypsy in England, he came to Christ as a boy. Gypsy Smith used to preach up and down this country. I remember Dr. H. A. Ironside saying that Gypsy Smith came to the Moody Church in Chicago on one occasion where he held meetings and told about his conversion and about his gypsy life. The people would sit entranced with the wonderful stories he told. At the end of the meeting he would give an altar call, and people would surge forward in great numbers. Dr. Ironside said he used to wonder why they were coming. Did they want to be gypsies, or what? They had really been given nothing in which to believe. I so well recall Dr. Lewis Sperry Chafer, my great teacher at Dallas

Seminary, saying to us in class, "Men, remember, you have never preached the gospel until you have given people something to believe, something God has done that their minds can grasp, something they can use as a basis for understanding what God has offered to them—their salvation."

Behind the belief, Paul says, is a message—something heard. "How can they believe in the one of whom they have not heard?" Something has to be preached. Some message must come. Again, this is an important aspect of Christian faith. These days we are hearing much of isms and asms and spasms that are coming into being, new cults springing up on every side, dominating the religious field. Often they make their appeal to some mystical feeling or philosophy, some idea men have of what could work.

But the glory of Christianity is that its message is grounded in history. It is objective truth, not just something that happens inside of you. It is not some feeling you are following that you hope will work out; it is the story of historic events. One of these events is the coming of Jesus as a baby in the manger of Bethlehem, followed by the arrival of the wise men from the east and the uproar that it caused in the kingdom of Judea, beginning with Herod the king himself. That is all part of history. Then there was the crucifixion and the resurrection and the events that followed in the church. These are all historic events—objective truth. The Christian faith is grounded in events that cannot be explained away. That is our message.

Human Messengers

Behind the message, of course, is the messenger. "How can they hear without someone preaching to them?" There has to be a messenger speaking forth this message. I believe God has always used some object or person to convey truth and that this method will never be superceded. All the marvelous machinery and inventions we have today—the communication media—are only ways of conveying the preaching of the Word of God. You can preach today on television, on radio, on cassette tapes, and on video tapes. You can have the message flung up to satellites and back to the four corners of the earth. But in every event, someone has to deliver the message. God has chosen preaching as his means of conveying this great truth in every generation.

That is why I don't believe the distribution of the written Scriptures alone will ever be sufficient to win men. Now, I do not demean that ministry, because it is an important one. The translating of the Word of God and the spreading of the Scriptures all over the earth are important. But they are only supplementary. That, alone, will never reach and change nations as does the gospel when proclaimed by a human messenger. God has sent men out everywhere, therefore, to preach this Word and to proclaim the truth.

Behind the messenger, as Paul then brings out, is the sender. "How can they preach unless they are sent?" There need be no doubt as to the One who does the sending. Jesus himself said, "Pray the Lord of the harvest, that he may send forth laborers." It is God who sends men. The great initiative in the process of redeeming men and women, healing them and restoring them, healing the fragmentation of their lives, is the great heart of the God who sends men out. He calls out men and women and sends them into the far reaches of the earth.

Paul has surely brought all this before us so that we might understand what a wonderful and beautiful thing God has done. That is why Paul quotes Isaiah here: "How beautiful are the feet of those who bring good news!" What a welcome and beautiful thing it is to think of God sending out men and women all over the earth with this message. How marvelous it is when this message takes root in the human heart! We never forget the ones who bring it to us. "How beautiful are the feet. . . ." Feet are not usually the most beautiful part of the body, but even they become beautiful when the message is conveyed and God delivers, frees, and heals us—and makes us whole.

I have often thought that calling on the name of the Lord is like turning on a light switch. You flick the switch on the

wall and the lights go on. It seems like such a simple thing.
Yet behind it is a complicated process. There are the trans-
mission towers, the substations, the dam built to hold back
the water, the poles on which the wires are strung—a tremendous complexity lies behind the simple act of turning
on a light switch. Every time you do it, power surges forth—
but it comes only because of that complicated process.

Every time an individual comes to the place where in
quietness he calls out to the Lord, a tremendous process is
behind it. There is the birth at Bethlehem, the darkness and
anguish of the mystery of the cross, the wonder and miracle
of the resurrection, the sending forth of the Holy Spirit on
the day of Pentecost—all this is the process behind a single
individual when he calls on the name of the Lord. God is
behind it, he has started it. The apostle wants us to understand this activity of the sovereign character of God.

Puzzle of Unbelief

But what if all this is provided, but still men do not respond? That is the problem Paul is facing here, with regard
to Israel:

> But not all the Israelites responded to the good news. For
> Isaiah says, "Lord, who has believed our message?" Conse-
> quently, faith comes from hearing the message, and the mes-
> sage is heard through the word of Christ (vv. 16,17).

Paul is telling us here that a strange reaction occurs when
people hear this message. It is what we might call the puzzle of unbelief. Isn't it strange how some people seem to
be so suspicious, so self-dependent, that even when good
news comes they don't want to receive it? Preachers and
others who tell the good news run into this reaction all the
time.

A young friend living in Fresno, California, once told me
the story of his conversion. He was a man of considerable
wealth, and he tried to reach his friends for Christ after he
himself became a Christian. With tremendous enthusiasm
he told them what had happened to him, how the Lord had

changed his whole life and saved his marriage. But he found that for the most part his words fell on deaf ears. His wealthy friends patted him on the back and went on their way.

Finally he decided on a rather strange and remarkable demonstration—both for his sake and the sake of his friends. He sat down and wrote out a check for a million dollars (and he was good for it, too!). Then he took his check around to his friends and said, "I have always regarded you highly as a friend. I have always wanted to do something for you. Would you receive this check as a gift from me?" People would look at the check and when they saw the amount of it, they would hand it back and say, "I can't take that from you." He tried to give that check out to a dozen or more of his friends and no one would take it, although it was a valid offer. Finally he faced the fact that there is something deeply embedded in human nature that does not want to hear good news, does not want to be helped too much, does not want to be the recipient of great riches without having some part in it.

Even the prophet Isaiah discovered this when he came to the people of Israel at a time in their history when they were surrounded by enemies. They were about to be overrun by the nations around them; they had turned to the idols of these nations. Degrading practices had come into the national life, and peace and joy had fled from the land. In these dark days, 725 years before Christ was born, Isaiah came and preached to this people good news about One who was coming. He said that on the basis of this person's life and death, God would work on their behalf. But he had to confess, as Paul brings out here, that they would not believe his message.

The great and luminous fifty-third chapter of Isaiah begins with those words:

Lord, who has believed our message? [and then continues]
And to whom has the arm of the Lord been revealed?
And he grew up before them like a young plant,
    and like a root out of dry ground;

> he had no form or comeliness that we should look at him,
>   and no beauty that we should desire him.
> He was despised and rejected by men;
>   a man of sorrows and acquainted with grief;
> and as one from whom men hid their faces
>   he was despised, and we esteemed him not.
> Surely he has borne our grief
>   and carried our sorrows;
> yet we esteemed him stricken,
>   smitten by God, and afflicted.
> But he was wounded for our transgressions,
>   he was bruised for our iniquities;
> upon him was the chastisement that made us whole,
>   and with his stripes we are healed.
> All we like sheep have gone astray;
>   we have turned every one to his own way;
> and the Lord has laid on him
>   the iniquity of us all.

Yet the nation of Israel said no to that tremendous revelation of Isaiah the prophet—at least, most of the Israelites did.

Now Paul isolates the difficulty for us in verse 71: "Consequently, faith comes from hearing the message, and the message is heard through the word of Christ." This, by the way, is a more accurate translation than the Authorized Version, which says, "and hearing comes by the word of God." It is really the word of Christ. Paul says that faith is aroused by hearing. If you hear a message, then you either have to believe it or disbelieve it. Your faith is aroused by the message. But if it is to be saving faith, he says, it must be a word about Christ. All Scripture is about Christ as Jesus himself said, "You search the Scriptures . . . and they bear testimony to me."

Once again, Paul sets Jesus right at the center of the universe. He is the very issue of life. Even back in ancient Israel, when they heard the news about Jesus it precipitated the puzzle of unbelief. People refused it, and the word "refused" brings the whole project of God's enterprise to reach men to a point of failure.

Two Views of Messiah

I have already shared with you a section from a letter written by a rabbi to a boy of Jewish background who is now a Christian. In his letter the rabbi also explained the difference between what the Jews believe about the Messiah and what Christians believe, as he saw it. Perhaps you would be interested in his words:

> The Messiah question is central to Christianity. This is the hub around which their whole theology rotates. To make this your major concern is to play their game. We [Jews] have a belief in a messiah, but this is not too rigidly defined, nor of central concern. According to our belief, the messiah is a man, descended from the house of David, since God had promised not to replace the line of David with another, who will defeat the enemies of the Jews, restore the people to the land of Israel, rebuild the temple in Jerusalem, and reign there and introduce an era of peace. The advent of the messiah has to do with God's plan for actualizing his plans in the world.

This is the usual Jewish position regarding the Messiah. He was a man, not a divine Being; he was to come into history only to deliver the Jews from their oppressors, in fulfillment of the promises to Israel of leadership among the nations. But they ignore passages such as Isaiah 53 and others that speak of the suffering of the Messiah. The rabbi goes on,

> The situation is quite different for the Christian. He believes that nothing that man does can help. Man necessarily exists in a state of sin. Ethical living, obedience to God, goodness, all are of no avail. The only way that a man can get out of a state of damnation is to believe that Jesus is his Savior or Messiah (quite a different meaning for the word). Thus the whole purpose of religion is for man to be in Jesus i.e., to accept this belief in Jesus as his Savior.

Now, that betrays a considerable degree of understanding of the Christian position and of the gospel. To show how thoroughly he understands it, he goes on.

The Law [to a Christian] is not only ineffective, but unnecessary, because once one has accepted Jesus, one of the by-products is that he is essentially good and needs no direction from the Law. From this point of view, one of the most basic and almost exclusive concerns of religion is the Messiah. Don't be shifted to that question without realizing the difference in import and meaning that places messiah, as used by a Jew, and Messiah, as used by a Christian, worlds apart.

This is the position that Jews still take today regarding Christ. Paul says that is the issue.

Nature's Witness

Well, someone may say, "The trouble is that the Jews never really heard the gospel. Maybe the problem is that it never reached them!" This brings up the question about those who never hear. Paul takes this up in verse 18:

But I ask, did they not hear? [His answer:] Of course they did:
> "Their voice has gone out into all the earth,
> their words to the ends of the world."

Psalm 19, from which Paul quotes here, is the great psalm that details nature's witness to God. It begins with the words,

> The heavens are telling the glory of God;
> and the firmament proclaims his handiwork.
> Day to day pours forth speech
> and night to night declares knowledge.
> There is no speech, nor are there words:
> their voice is not heard;
> yet their voice goes out through all the earth,
> and their words to the end of the world.

There has been a universal proclamation of the gospel through nature. This is not a lot of light about God, but it is light. In the first chapter of Romans Paul mentioned this witness:

> . . . what may be known about God is plain to them. For since the creation of the world God's invisible qualities—his eternal power and divine nature—have been clearly seen, being understood from what has been made, so that men are without excuse (1:19,20).

This is the answer to the question, "What about those who have never heard about God?" There aren't any people who have never heard about God! Everywhere men and women know something about God. He is revealed in nature. There is a universal proclamation that has gone out. And if it is observed, if it is noticed and followed, more light will be given. This is why Hebrews 11, that great faith chapter, gives us the simplest declaration of how men come to God:

> Without faith it is impossible to please God, because anyone who comes to him must believe that he exists and that he rewards those who earnestly seek him (v. 6).

First, there must be belief, or faith. Then one must believe that God is, and that he rewards men who diligently seek him. So all men everywhere are responsible to seek the God who is revealed in nature. They may have no more light than that, but if they are obedient to it that is enough to bring them, through gradually dawning light, to the knowledge of Christ. God will see to it that they have further light. And Israel had that proclamation. No matter how low they sank in their understanding, no matter how dark it became in the land, they at least had that universal proclamation of truth that would have brought them back to truth and to God.

But that isn't all. There is another stage of the revelation of God. God, in his grace, often gives more light even when people refuse the light of nature. No one deserves more light, but God gives it nevertheless. I think the United States of America, above all nations, ought to be grateful for the grace of God that has poured light out upon us when we did not deserve it. God has given us much light. But we must remember that more light does not necessarily mean more belief. To turn up the light brighter does not mean that people are going to believe more than when it was dim. Unbelief can reject bright light as well as dim light, so more light does not necessarily mean more belief. That is why the U.S.A., with this great and shining light pouring so brilliantly upon it, is still a nation filled with unbelievers as was Israel of old.

Beyond that revelation of God in nature, God sends messengers:

> Again I ask, did Israel not understand? First, Moses says,
> "I will make you envious by means of
> those who are not a nation;
> I will make you angry by a nation that
> has no understanding."
> Then Isaiah boldly says,
> "I was found by those who did not seek me;
> I revealed myself to those who did not ask for
> me" (Rom. 10:19,20).

God sent the prophets to Israel. He sent Moses and Samuel, Elijah and Elisha, Isaiah and Jeremiah, and all the other prophets of the Old Testament. Through many years and centuries he sent them to this people—and he did it to arouse them to jealousy through the fact that although Israel often rejected the prophets, the nations around would believe them. This would be true more fully in the day when the Gentile nations would suddenly turn to God in large numbers while the Jews remained obdurate in their unbelief.

This, of course, is exactly what has happened in history. Paul singles out the specific principle here that God uses to arouse belief, even when people tend to reject truth—jealousy. I was watching my grandson play with his cousins the other day. He was playing with a certain toy until he became tired of it and threw it away. One of his cousins picked it up and started playing with it, and immediately the little boy ran over and grabbed the toy away. "No, that's mine!" he said. He wanted to play with it only because he was made jealous by someone else having it. Certainly God understands this principle in fallen human nature. He even uses it at times to make people wake up. This is why God pours out blessings upon an individual or a family, with one member of the family receiving spiritual insight. He does it to make the others jealous so they will listen to him. This is why God will pour out blessings upon one nation to make other nations jealous. "What is the secret of your blessing?" they will ask. Thus they might hear the witness about God.

If you understand some of these things you will be able to read your newspapers differently than you ordinarily do. What is God doing in the human events of our day? We see them as simply a conflict of warring factions of humanity. But God is using these events to arouse people to jealousy. Paul gives two instances of this:

First, he points out what Moses said—that God would use a people far less intelligent than the Jews. One of the striking things about Jewish history is the brilliance of the Jews. It would be impossible to list the many Jewish leaders in the fields of science, philosophy, literature, art, and music in our day. They dominate the field. Over 12 percent of the Nobel Prize winners have been Jewish. And yet, these brilliant people, with their tremendous minds, are often confronted with people, savages in the jungles, untaught, dark, and clouded in their thinking, who find God and become Christians and are delivered from evil and given blessings, hope, peace, and even prosperity. God is doing this only to arouse his people and awaken them.

Then Isaiah came along. Not only will God use those who are less intelligent, he says, but God will use people who are less motivated: "I was found by those who did not seek me. I revealed myself to those who did not ask for me." Another characteristic of the Jew has been his zeal for God, as Paul has already pointed out. And yet, careless Gentiles, who are not even thinking about God very often, learn through Christ to revel in the grace and love and blessing of the living God. This is all to arouse the Jews to jealousy. God uses this principle with Gentiles, too. That is why people watch Christians. There is blessing there that the non-Christian can't understand. God is trying to use it to awaken them to listen. that they might be saved, to turn and settle the issue at the feet of Jesus.

Four Thousand Year Day

A final stage of divine pursuit is described in verse 21:

But concerning Israel he says, "All day long I have held out my hands to a disobedient and obstinate people."

What a beautiful picture of the character of God. Here is his patience—all day long! That day has stretched now for almost four thousand years of human history. Four thousand years ago Abraham set out for Canaan. Four thousand years later, God is still holding out his hands to this stubborn people, wanting to draw them to himself.

He is not only patient, but loving. He holds out his hands. This is the stance of God toward those who resist his will—with wide open arms, all day long he is waiting to draw them back.

Remember how Jesus put it to the Pharisees of his day? "You will not come unto me that you may have life." And looking over the city of Jerusalem, he wept as he saw the stubbornness and the pride of people who will not admit their need. This is being repeated again and again throughout the world today. God longs to draw men to himself. He must somehow arouse faith in the individual. To do so, he sends messengers with a tremendous message, and still there is resistance to the will and purpose of God. So the chapter closes with this picture of God standing with his arms open, longing to draw men to himself, stating that the problem is a disobedient and obstinate people.

I think the most amazing thing from this account is to realize that in order to perish, i.e., to go to hell, you must resist the pleas of a loving God. God never damns anyone to hell without a chance. Don't ever let anyone tell you the Bible teaches that. The Bible does not teach any such thing. Rather, it teaches us that no one, not one person, will end up separated from God who has not personally resisted the claim and appeal of a loving God who sought to reach them.

5

There's Hope Ahead

The eleventh chapter of Romans deals very strongly with Israel—its hope, its promises, and its relationship to the church. Unfortunately, the church and Israel are often like two relatives who can't get along with each other. Through the centuries, disagreement and outright persecution have prevailed between Jews and Christians. But Romans 11 gives us some helpful insights into how to live with our Jewish friends and neighbors.

Twice in this passage the apostle Paul asks the question, "Did God reject his people?" That is, is God through with Israel because of their rejection of the person of Jesus and the crucifixion and resurrection of Christ? Because they turned a deaf ear to that, has God wiped them out? Has he said they no longer have any place in his scheme of things?

Both times Paul answers that question, "By no means!" God is not through with the Jews. Anyone who teaches that the church has now inherited all the promises of Israel had better take a second look at the Scriptures, especially Romans 11. It is amazing how many people apply all the blessings and glories promised to Israel in the Old Testament to the church, but they unfairly apply all the cursings and the

punishments to Israel! Let's take a look at Paul's answer to
the question, "Does God reject his people?"

> I ask then, Did God reject his people? By no means! I am an
> Israelite myself, a descendant of Abraham, from the tribe of
> Benjamin. God did not reject his people, whom he foreknew
> (Rom. 11:1,2).

Those among the Jews whom God foreknew, he did not reject. Paul is the great example of that. Here we have clear
evidence that God has never set aside the Jews, in respect
to individual salvation. Through all the Christian centuries
Jews have been coming to Christ, coming back to God, coming into the fulfillment of the promise of Abraham by faith
in Jesus Christ.

Notice how Paul refers to himself as one of those fore-
known, i.e., one of the elect, one whom God has set aside
to be his. In the letter to the Galatians the apostle reminds
us that this was done from his mother's womb, so that all
through those years of resistance and pharisaical anger at
the claims of Jesus, when Paul was persecuting the church
and "breathing out threatenings and slaughters," he was
nevertheless one of the elect. Though he was struggling, he
was one whom God was inexorably drawing to himself—
and Paul never forgot that. In many of his letters he marvels
at the grace of God that took him, a blasphemer and per-
secutor of the church, and changed his heart, making him
into a new creature in Christ. He is but one example of the
many thousands of Jews through the centuries who have believed in Christ.

But even that does not exhaust the position of Israel in
God's program. Not only do some Jews become Christian,
but there are many who remain Jews who nevertheless are
perhaps born again, saved individuals. Paul cites an example
from the prophet Elijah:

> Don't you know what the Scripture says in the passage about
> Elijah—how he appealed to God against Israel: "Lord, they
> have killed your prophets and torn down your altars; I am the

only one left, and they are trying to kill me"? And what was God's answer to him? "I have reserved for myself seven thousand who have not bowed the knee to Baal." So too, at the present time there is a remnant chosen by grace. And if by grace, then it is no longer by works; if it were, grace would no longer be grace (vv. 2–6).

There was a time in the life of the prophet Elijah when he thought he was the only one left. It was after that tremendous encounter with the priests of Baal, recorded in 1 Kings 18, when fire came down from heaven and consumed the sacrifices. Queen Jezebel mounted a persecution against the prophets of God, including Elijah, and brought Elijah to the place where he felt that he was the only one left.

Broken Computer

Have you ever felt like that? "O Lord, they have all left you. I'm the only one left. I'm the only one who's faithful." That was how Elijah felt. But God said, "Elijah, your computer is broken. You only see one left; I see seven thousand who have not yet bowed the knee to Baal. I have kept them from it. I have reserved to myself seven thousand who have not bowed the knee to Baal."

Like many of us, Elijah made mistakes. *First*, he forgot about man's limited knowledge about any subject. We don't see very clearly; we don't understand all the issues. It is never as bad as it looks, no matter how bad it gets in these coming years—and it may get bad. But it will never be as bad as it looks, because our knowledge does not encompass all the ones who remain faithful.

Second, Elijah forgot about God's unlimited power. The situation is never as bad as it looks because God is never as weak as he seems. Sometimes we think God must have lost the battle, that the powers of darkness are so strong and violent and so in command that God has given up. But when we think that way, we have forgotten what the Scriptures tell us again and again—that God is using the very opposi-

tion of the enemy to bring about his purposes. Never forget
that. God cannot lose because he uses the very opposition
against him to win. Elijah had no reason to despair.

Third, Elijah forgot about life's unmixable principles. If
salvation is by grace, then it can't be by works. And if it is
by works, then it can't be by grace. Grace, you see, is God
at work. Works is man at work. We think we have to earn
our way to heaven. I find this revealed in the thinking even
of many Christians. A man said to me the other day, "Why
should this happen to me? What have I done that I should
have to go through this kind of trial?" I realized that I had
said the same thing not long before. I really thought that I
had put God in my debt, that I had somehow earned something, and deserved something better from him. Now, that
is works, and Paul reminds us here that you cannot mix
works and grace. If God is going to call you and save you
and deliver you, then it is not going to depend on your
works. As James points out, your works will be there if your
faith is real, because it is faith that produces works. But the
works are not the saving factor. That is what Elijah forgot.

So there were thousands in Paul's day, and there are
thousands of Jews today, who perhaps have never really
heard about Jesus. I think there are many Jews today who
are earnest, devout, humble souls, trusting in the Old Testament record. They have never heard anything about Jesus
that would make them feel that he really is their Messiah.
And yet they have believed what is revealed in the Old
Testament about the Messiah. There are probably thousands
of Jews today who are still faithful believers in the only bit
of Christ that they know—that which is revealed in the Old
Testament. Are they not a part of this "remnant of grace"?
Paul seems to suggest this.

Results of Unbelief

At any rate, Paul has made it clear that God is not reject-
ing individuals out of Israel. And yet the majority are turning away:

What then? What Israel sought so earnestly it did not obtain,
but the elect did. The others were hardened, as it is written:
  "God gave them a spirit of stupor,
      eyes so that they could not see
      and ears so that they could not hear,
      to this very day."
And David says,
    "May their table become a snare and a trap,
      a stumbling block and a retribution for them.
    May their eyes be darkened so that they cannot see,
      and their backs be bent forever" (vv. 7–10).

Now those are horrible words, but they represent the reaction that God has determined should accompany unbelief.
When you hear truth, it is always important to do something
about it. If you know something is true, then you had better
act on it. If you don't, you lose your capacity to recognize
truth. Gradually the dry rot described here, so visible among
many in Israel today, will set in. Paul calls it a blindness.
Their eyes are blinded, so that even when the truth is there
they cannot see it. Their ears are deaf. Even when loving
appeals and warnings are set before them, they don't hear
them.

Their table [their food], becomes a snare and a trap, leading into slavery. The food of Israel referred to here is the
Law, the Scriptures. Jews highly value the Law. Now many
don't know a lot about it. Many Jews today are hardly ac-
quainted with anything in the Old Testament. The rabbis
have given themselves to the study of it, and yet all that
intensive study only seems to make them sink deeper and
deeper into the trap of legalistic slavery. They are bound by
rituals and spend their days constantly working out inter-
pretative details.

Not long ago I was reading about Dr. Joseph Goebbels,
the propaganda minister among the Nazis, who, on one occasion, asked a Jewish rabbi to teach him how the Jews
approached the Scriptures. "I understand that you Jews
have a peculiar way of reasoning when you come to the
Talmud and the Torah (the Old Testament), and I want
you to teach it to me." The rabbi said, "I'm sorry, but you're

too old for that." "What do you mean?" he asked. "Well,"
the rabbi told him, "we have three questions we ask a boy
before he enters into the study of the Talmud. If he can
answer them, we let him into the study. If he can't, he has
no chance." Goebbels said, "Ask them of me. What's the first
question?"

Who Washes?

The rabbi said, "The first question is this: Two men fall
down a chimney; one comes out clean and the other is dirty,
which one washes?" Dr. Goebbels replied, "Oh, that's easy.
The dirty one washes, of course." The rabbi said, "Wrong.
It is the clean one who washes." "How do you reason that?"
The rabbi answered, "When they fall down the chimney,
they look at each other, and the dirty one sees the clean one,
so he thinks he is clean, too; but the clean one sees the dirty
one and thinks he is dirty, so he washes." "All right," Goebbels said, "there is a strange logic about that. But give me
the second question."

"The second question is this: Two men fall down a chimney. One comes out dirty, and the other clean. Which one
washes?" Goebbels replied, "That's the same question." "No
it isn't, it's an entirely different question." "Well," Goebbels
went on, "I think I can answer that. It is the clean one who
washes." The rabbi said, "Wrong. They look at each other.
The dirty one looks at the clean one and says, 'Isn't it wonderful that two men can fall down a chimney and come out
clean?' But the dirty man holds up his hands and sees that
they are dirty. So he washes."

Goebbels asked, "What's the third question?" "Two men
fall down a chimney . . ." Goebbels interrupted, "That's the
same one!" "No, it isn't," the rabbi replied, "it's an entirely
different problem! What's the answer?" Goebbels said, "I
don't know." The rabbi pointed out, "Neither of them wash
because it is a ridiculous story to begin with! How could
two men fall down a chimney and one come out dirty and
the other clean? So unless a boy can answer those questions,
we never admit him to the Talmud."

It is this kind of strange, penetrating, and yet difficult reasoning that accounts for much of Jewish unbelief. In a paper printed and distributed by Jewish rabbis in which the differences between Christianity and Judaism are described, one rabbi writes about Paul:

> Paul claimed that obedience to the Torah (the Law) could not guarantee salvation; rather, salvation was obtainable only through acceptance of and faith in Christ Jesus. To believe that a person could atone for his own sinful condition through any efforts on his own, as, for example, by obeying the laws of the Torah, was accordingly a delusion. But Paul eagerly announced that what man could not himself accomplish, namely salvation, could still be accomplished for him. Only God, however, was powerful enough to atone for man's sinfulness, and Paul held that the death of Christ Jesus was that act of divine atonement.

Then he adds,

> We Jews have rejected this Gentile Christian view. Judaism, as shaped by our rabbis in Palestine, conceived of the body as a gift of God, and to this day we regard the body as holy and wholesome, not as a prison from which to escape. Any inclination by man to commit a wrongdoing, we hold, resides not in his body but in his heart or mind. And this inclination can be overcome by a change of heart or mind. Thus man, by himself, does indeed possess the power to atone for his own misdeeds, and we Jews have, in our Torah, the guidance directing our hearts and minds to righteous living.

On that basis, the Jews say, they can win their way to acceptance before God without dealing with the sin problem and without ever taking into consideration the full teaching of the Scriptures. Paul says, therefore, that many have been rejected because of that.

Now he takes up the second question:

> Again I ask, Did they stumble so as to fall beyond recovery? Not at all! (v. 11)

If you have read the Book of Acts, you know that everywhere Paul went he began his ministry with the Jews. It was

only when the Jews refused to hear that he would turn to
the Gentiles. So, in all these cities, the Gentiles were blessed
and enriched by his ministry only because the Jews had refused it. Gentiles were allowed to believe and to become
different people to make the Jews jealous.

We Christians ought to be so alive, so vital in our Christianity, so excited and full of joy and love toward one another that every Jew we contact will say to himself, "How
come they have it and we don't? How come they have a
light on their faces and joy and love in their hearts?" We
have to hang our heads in shame and admit that through the
centuries there has been very little in the church to attract
the jealousy of Israel. It has been the other way around. But
Paul says this was God's intention, that the Gentiles should
become so alive as to awaken the Jews.

Paul's second argument is that Israel must ultimately return to God because world-wide blessing will come only
when that happens:

> But if their transgression means riches for the world, and their
> loss means riches for the Gentiles, how much greater riches
> will their fullness bring! I am talking to you Gentiles. Inasmuch
> as I am the apostle to the Gentiles, I make much of my minis-
> try in the hope that I may somehow arouse my own people to
> envy and save some of them. For if their rejection is the recon-
> ciliation of the world, what will their acceptance be, but life
> from the dead? (vv. 12–15)

When I was at the Congress for World Evangelization at
Lausanne, Switzerland, in 1974, I was moved to see that
every nation on earth was represented there. The riches
of the gospel had in some way penetrated every nation on
the face of the earth. Those riches really speak not of material prosperity, but of freedom, the human spirit made free.
It is a fact today that everywhere the gospel is freely proclaimed, you have a free people. But where it is resisted or
rejected or ignored, you have people drifting into violence,
anarchy, exploitation, and tyranny. This is because human
freedom comes by means of the gospel. We in the Gentile

world ought to give thanks to God for the riches that have come our way because of the blindness of Israel.

But Paul's argument is this: if that kind of riches has come because of the Jews' rejection, what will it be like in the day when Israel comes again into its proper position? According to the prophets, that is the time when the earth will blossom like the rose, when there will be no more war, "nothing to hurt or destroy in all God's holy mountain." Israel is the key. This is why every Christian should keep his eye on that remarkable people and see what is happening to them.

The First Handful

Paul's third argument is found in verse 16:

> If the part of the dough offered as firstfruits is holy, then the whole batch is holy; if the root is holy, so are the branches.

Now, it would take a good Jew to really understand this. Paul is referring to the offerings and sacrifices in the tabernacle. For the offering of the firstfruits, a pile of dough was made up, and the priest would take a handful of it and present it to God. Paul's argument is that if that first handful was acceptable and holy before God, the rest of the dough would be, too. Now, the firstfruits here is Abraham, the father of the nation of Israel. Abraham was accepted before God; therefore his true descendants will be, too. They are not cut off from God or from his relationship with them; they are claimed by God. The God who made Abraham holy, by faith, is able to make his descendants holy, too, when they exercise the faith of Abraham.

Paul's fourth argument has to do with the olive tree:

> If some of the branches have been broken off, and you, though a wild shoot, have been grafted in among the others and now share in the nourishing sap from the olive root, do not boast over those branches. If you do, consider this: You do not support the root, but the root supports you. You will say then,

"Branches were broken off so that I could be grafted in."
Granted. But they were broken off because of unbelief, and
you stand by faith. Do not be arrogant, but be afraid. For if
God did not spare the natural branches, he will not spare you
either (vv. 17–21).

Once again Abraham is symbolized by the olive tree. The
New Testament tells us that when a Gentile becomes a
Christian, he also becomes a son of Abraham. He, in a sense,
becomes an Israelite. But when a Jew becomes a Christian,
he doesn't have to become a Gentile. You see, the natural
fruit of the olive tree is the Jews. It is we Gentiles who are
grafted in.

C. S. Lewis put it this way: "In a sense, the converted
Jew is the only normal human being in the world." What
do you think of that? He goes on, "Everyone else is, from
one point of view, a special case dealt with under emergency
conditions." That's how we got in. God opened the back
door and let us in as an emergency case. But the ones who
really belong are the Jews. It is healthy for Gentile Christians to remember that. The Jews are not hanging around
waiting for us to be nice to them. It is they who have been
nice to us. We ought to remember that and respond with
gratitude and humility to what God has done in placing us
in this olive tree.

Paul's last argument is found in verses 22–24:

Consider therefore the kindness and sternness of God: sternness
to those who fell, but kindness to you, provided that you continue in his kindness. Otherwise, you also will be cut off. And
if they do not persist in unbelief, they will be grafted in, for
God is able to graft them in again. After all, if you were cut
out of an olive tree that is wild by nature, and contrary to
nature were grafted into a cultivated olive tree, how much
more readily will these, the natural branches, be grafted into
their own olive tree?

The olive tree signifies the faith of Abraham, the position
of receiving blessing from the God of the earth through
sheer grace, without any merit on our part. According to

Paul here, we who were like a wild olive tree, with hard, shriveled, bitter fruit, were taken and grafted into this rich olive tree. But that is contrary to what happens in nature.

If you take a nectarine branch and graft it into a peach tree, what does the branch grow from then on—peaches or nectarines? It still grows nectarines. The fruit is determined by the branch, not by the tree. The peach tree will grow nectarines on a nectarine branch, and plums on a plum branch, and so on. That is what happens according to nature. Following Paul's analogy here, if we, a wild olive branch, were grafted into a rich, cultivated olive tree, the fruit that would continue to grow on the branch would be wild olives, bitter and shriveled.

But God does a miracle with us. He changes us so the fruit that comes forth is the fruit of the Spirit, and we begin to produce the rich, wonderful, fat fruit of the good olive tree in our lives. Again, Paul argues, if God can do that with bitter fruit such as we Gentile believers are, how much more will he produce richness with the true branches?

How God Appears to You

Then Paul speaks of the kindness and the severity of God. If you come to God needy and repentant, acknowledging that you need help, you will always find him to be a loving, gracious, open-armed, open-hearted Sovereign, ready to help you, ready to forgive you, ready to give you all that you need. But if you come to God complaining, excusing yourself, justifying what you've been doing and trying to make it look good in his sight, you will always find that God is as hard as iron, and as merciless as fire, as stern as a judge. God will invariably turn that face toward those who come in pride and self-justification.

This is the secret of the mystery of Israel and its blindness today. As long as the Jews come to God in self-justification they always find a hard, iron-willed, stern God. But, as Zechariah the prophet describes, when Jesus appears and they look at him whom they had pierced, they will ask him,

"Where did you get those wounds in your hands?" He will say, "These are those which I received in the house of my friends." Then they will mourn for him as one mourns for an only child, and the mourning of Israel that day will be like the mourning for Hadadriminon in the plains of Megiddo. The whole nation will mourn. Then God will take that nation and bless them, and they will replenish the earth.

This is surely a reminder to our own hearts of the faithfulness of God. His promises will not fail. God's purposes will never be shortchanged. God is going to accomplish all that he says he will do. Though it may be a long way around, and though it may lead through many trials, temptations, hurts, and heartaches, what God has said he will do, he will carry through.

6

Our Great and Glorious God

In the first part of Romans 11 Paul has given us five reasons why it is evident that God has not forgotten his people the Jews. *First*, he desires to arouse Israel to jealousy. God is reaching Gentiles because he wants ultimately to reach Jews. *Second*, Paul says the promises of world-wide blessing that fill so many prophetic passages of the Old Testament hinge upon the restoration of Israel to God. World-wide blessing can never come until Israel is back in right relationship with its God. *Third*, he says that if the patriarchs, Abraham and Isaac and Jacob, could be made holy by God, then God is able to make Jews holy after thousands of years have passed. Therefore there is hope for Israel.

In Paul's *fourth* argument he uses the figure of an olive tree. The natural branches of the tree, the Jews, are broken off and unnatural branches, the Gentiles, are grafted on. Jews who become Christians today are "completed Jews," but Gentiles who become Christians become spiritual Jews. Therefore, *fifth*, if God could take a twisted, deformed Gentile and make him into a son of the living God, how much more can he do this with the natural branches, the Jews!

Supernatural Resistance

This brings us to verse 25, where Paul actually prophesies the restoration that is coming to Israel. Up to now he has been arguing this from reason, but now he prophesies the restoration directly:

> I do not want you to be ignorant of this mystery, brothers, so that you may not be conceited: Israel has experienced a hardening in part until the full number of the Gentiles has come in. And so all Israel will be saved, as it is written:
> "The deliverer will come from Zion;
>   he will turn godlessness away from Jacob.
> And this is my covenant with them
>   when I take away their sins."
> As far as the gospel is concerned, they are enemies on your account; but as far as election is concerned, they are loved on account of the patriarchs, for God's gifts and his call are irrevocable (vv. 25–29).

Perhaps the striking thing about this passage is that Paul calls the Jews' present resistance to the gospel a mystery. He does not mean that it is obscure and difficult to understand. The word "mystery," in Scripture, refers to something supernatural. It is not brought about by natural causes.

If you have had any occasion to try to witness to a Jew, perhaps you have run up against what seemed to be a rock wall of indifference to what you were trying to say. That resistance may well have been what Paul is talking about here, a strange hardening toward the gospel on the part of the Jews. This hardening, which Paul calls a mystery, cannot be explained by the normal reasons for resistance to the gospel. He says three things about this that we must take care to notice. First, it is a hardening "in part." That is, not all Jews are afflicted this way. We are not told here how much of Israel is going to be hardened. All we are told is that some Jews will not hear, will not receive the gospel. Whether the one you are talking to is hardened or not is difficult to determine. It is often the case that the person needs to be witnessed to and loved over a period of time. No one can say that any given person belongs to that hardening. But we can say that there will be, as has been evident in history, a strange, remarkable resistance to the gospel by the Jews.

Not only does Paul say this hardening is in part, but it is also limited in duration: "until the full number of the Gentiles come in." So they are not bound to experience this forever. What does "the full number of the Gentiles" mean? I really do not like that translation. The word the apostle uses is "the fullness of the Gentiles." Well, what does that mean?

Some, as in this version, have interpreted it to mean a certain number of Gentiles will be converted. God has a certain number in mind and he is going to let the gospel go out to all the world until that number of Gentiles has been converted, and then he will release Israel from its blindness, its hardness. But I do not think this refers to a certain number.

Actually, this is the second time in chapter 11 that the word "fullness" is used. It is used not only of the Gentiles, but also of the Jews. In verse 12 Paul says of Israel, "But if their transgression means riches for the world, and their loss means riches for the Gentiles, how much greater riches will their fullness bring?" There is the same word, *pleroma,* which means that which fills. Notice that it is set in direct contrast to the words "their loss" or "their fall." That refers to the time when Israel was driven out of Jerusalem by the armies of the Romans in A.D. 70 and scattered throughout all the nations of the earth.

Restored Spiritual Riches

This "loss" does not mean there is a diminished number of Jews. The Jews have increased in number throughout all these centuries of dispersion. Paul is talking, rather, about diminished spiritual riches. The Jews have lost the quality and richness of their relationship with God. Though they have the outward trappings of faith and the very books of the Law, still they have lost that richness of relationship that sets the heart aglow and the face radiant with the light, love, beauty, and grace, and character of God. This is the loss; therefore "the fullness" means the restoration of these riches. So, when Paul uses this phrase, "the fullness of the Gentiles," he is talking about a Gentile church so spiritually rich that it will awaken again the envy of Israel.

Anyone who reads church history knows there has not been a great deal in Gentile churches that would awaken the Jews to envy! They see enemies, for the most part, among Gentile Christians. Oftentimes the Jews have been oppressed, persecuted, and terribly treated—all in the name of Jesus Christ—by those who profess to be Christians. But I think Paul is saying a very hopeful thing here; a day is coming when the Gentile churches will be enriched with such spiritual blessing that the Jews will say, "We should have that! That's the way we should be!" And the Jews will be open, as never before, to the gospel of the grace of God.

I think we are seeing a taste of this now. This is one reason why Jews, in greater number than ever before since the time of the dispersion, have been open to the gospel and turning to Christ. This is an amazing and encouraging thing. This is what the apostle says must take place.

Paul then says the prophets have told us this is going to happen: "The deliverer will come from Zion; he will turn godlessness away from Jacob." That is a promise in the Old Testament. Furthermore, quoting from Jeremiah, he says, "And this is my covenant with them when I take away their sins." The deliverer is coming and forgiveness is going to be granted to Israel. That is clearly stated in the prophets. So the apostle closes with two important things we ought to remember about the Jews: "As far as the gospel is concerned, they are enemies on your account; but as far as election is concerned, they are loved on account of the patriarchs, for God's gifts and his call are irrevocable" (vv. 28,29).

The Jews may treat you as an enemy, due to this strange supernatural hardening that has happened to part of Israel.

This has been the experience of many who have gone as missionaries to the Jews. They have been treated as though they were attacking the Jews instead of trying to minister to them and help them. They have aroused the enmity and anger of the Jews. I have heard the group called "Jews for Jesus" tell about going into Jewish communities to share and talk about their experience as Jews who have found the glory and the grace of God in Jesus Christ. They have met with violence and personal attack.

Any such missionary movement among the Jews seems to create consternation among Jewish ranks and extreme resentment. So remember, you may be treated as an enemy. But remember also that the Jews are loved by an unchanging God. God loves every Jew, without exception. No matter how stubborn or resistant they may be, he has set his love upon them. And the nations of the world had better not forget it. God still has chosen the Jews.

Bound to Disobedience

Now the apostle moves on to show us God's principle of salvation for all men:

Just as you who were at one time disobedient to God have now received mercy as a result of their disobedience, so they too, as a result of God's mercy to you, have now become disobedient in order that they too may now receive mercy. For God has bound all men over to disobedience so that he may have mercy on them all (vv. 30–32).

In this striking statement you see something of how the mind of God works and some of the strange wheels-within-wheels with which he moves in current history to bring about his purposes. Paul says that God used the Jews' disobedience, their rejection of their own Messiah, to give opportunity to rebellious Gentiles to receive mercy and grace from his hand. It was only by the Jews' disobedience that the gospel went out to the Gentiles.

That, by the way, answers again the question with which

this whole section begins. In Romans 9 Paul raises the question, "Has God failed?" Since he obviously has been trying to reach the Jews and has sent his own Son as their Messiah and they rejected him, does that mean God has failed? The answer is now clear, No, God has not failed. He used Jewish rejection as a means to reach the Gentile world, which he had intended to reach all along. That was his way of bringing it about.

Then, Paul adds, after having shown mercy to the Gentiles, God now uses the very mercies he has shown to the Gentiles to make the Jews angry and rebellious in order that they too can receive mercy. What Paul is saying here is that unless you realize how rebellious your heart is, there is no chance for you to receive mercy. So God works in human history to make us aware of our basic, inherent rebellion against him. Paul concludes that everyone is a rebel, and God desires that everyone admit it, so they can receive mercy.

What is the thing that keeps any individual or nation from receiving mercy from God? It is always a self-righteous, self-confident attitude. "I don't need help. I can handle it myself. I am able to handle all the problems of life on my own. I don't need God." Any individual or nation with that attitude has cut himself off from receiving the mercy of God, for without mercy there is no way we can ever fulfill our humanity. So God, as Paul puts it here, has "bound all men over to [the knowledge of their] disobedience so that he may have mercy upon them all."

The Deep Riches

Now all this awakens in the apostle's heart an outburst of praise and adoration for the wisdom and the greatness of God. He closes this section with these words:

> Oh, the depth of the riches, the wisdom and the
> knowledge of God!
> How unsearchable his judgments, and
> his paths beyond tracing out!

"Who has known the mind of the Lord?
    Or who has been his adviser?"
"Who has ever given to God,
    that God should repay him?"
For from him and through him and to him are
    all things.
To him be the glory forever! Amen (vv. 33–36).

This reminder of the strange ways God works awakens within the apostle a tremendous outburst of praise for God's inscrutable wisdom. As you look at these verses, you can see certain things that have stirred the apostle. There are the deep riches, as Paul calls them, of God's wisdom and his ways. They are beyond human exploration. There is no way we can finally fathom God.

God is greater than man. He is beyond us, and we must always remember that. Our minds cannot grasp the full greatness of God! We can understand what he tells us about himself, but beyond that, there is much more that we cannot know. There are depths of riches. That is why we are always being surprised by God. He is always enriching us in ways that we do not anticipate.

Then Paul speaks of God's "unsearchable judgments." These are "acts of God," such as droughts, which totally mystify the meteorologists, or earthquakes—anything God chooses—which come as a total surprise to men. Often we are baffled when these things occur. But God's ways are unsearchable. No man can call God to account and say, "You have no right to do that!" Though we do this all the time, we have no right to do it. For God is beyond us; he knows so much more than we do.

Paul then is impressed by the untraceable ways of God, the paths of God that are beyond understanding. We can't put it all together. We can believe it, but we can't explain it. For instance, it is clear from Scripture that nothing God ever planned interferes with human responsibility. Nothing God has ever said will in any way infringe on our free will or choice. We are free to make choices. We know it. We feel ourselves free to decide to do this or that, to do good or

bad. Nothing God ever plans interferes with that freedom of
human choice. And yet the striking thing is that nothing
humans ever do can frustrate God's sovereign plan. Isn't that
astonishing? How can you explain that? No matter what we
do, whether we choose this or that with the freedom of
choice we have, ultimately it all works out to accomplish
what God has determined shall be done. That is the kind of
God we have.

Searching Questions

Paul is not only impressed with God's inscrutable wisdom
and ways, but he contrasts it with the impotence of man.
He asks three searching questions. If you have trouble with
God's wisdom, try to answer his questions. His *first* one is,
"Who has known the mind of the Lord?" What he is asking
is, "Who has ever anticipated what God is going to do?"
Have you? Have you ever been able to figure out how God
is going to handle the situations you get into? Oh, we all
try, but it never turns out quite the way we think it will,
does it? There is a little twist to it that we never could have
guessed.

You see this in the case of Jesus. Remember how the
Pharisees asked him, "Should we pay taxes to Caesar?" They
thought they had him. If he said no, the Romans would be
angry at him; if he said yes, then the Jews would be angry
at him. Do you remember how he handled it? He called for
a coin and said, "Whose picture is on this coin?" They said,
"Caesar's." He said, "All right. What Caesar has put his
image on, you give to Caesar (i.e., pay your taxes); but
what God has put his image on, you give that to him." God
had put his image on men, and that is what they owed to
God—themselves. The Pharisees couldn't handle that kind
of answer. It wiped them out.

Remember the woman caught in adultery? Her stern and
self-righteous accusers were ready to put her to death. When
they brought her to Jesus, he didn't do a thing at first; he
just stooped and wrote on the ground. He looked up, finally,

and said, "He that is without sin among you, let him cast the first stone." They stood there, puzzled and transfixed, then every one of them began to think of other places they ought to be. Soon they were all gone, and no one was left except the woman and Jesus. How could you ever have anticipated that he would handle it that way? How unsearchable are his judgments! Who has anticipated what God is going to do? No one.

Second question: "Or who has been his adviser?"—in other words, "Who has ever suggested something that God has never thought of?" Have you ever tried that? I have. I have sometimes looked at a situation and saw the way to work it all out and suggested to God how he could do it. I thought I had been very helpful to him. But in the final outworking of the matter, it turned out that he knew things I didn't know and he was working at things I never saw and could not have seen. God's final outworking of it was right, and mine would have been wrong. So the question remains, "Who has ever suggested something to God that he has never thought of?"

Paul's *last* question is, "Who has ever given to God, that God should repay him?" That is, "Who has put God in his debt?" "Why," Paul says, "everything we are and have comes from him. He gives to us; we don't give to him." There is nothing we could give to God that he doesn't already own or have in abundance, or could make, if he had to! There is nothing. And so he concludes with this great outburst: "For from him and through him and to him are all things. To him be the glory forever! Amen."

God is the originator of all things; all things come from him. He is the sustainer of all things; they all depend on him. As C. S. Lewis puts it, "To argue with God is to argue with the very power that makes it possible to argue at all!" He is the end purpose of all. All things will find their culmination in God. He is the reason why all things exist. Therefore, "to him be the glory forever! Amen."

Then there occurs what must be the most terrible, tragic separation that has ever been made in the Bible. The chapter division here cuts off Paul's conclusion from all the tremendous arguments which have led up to it. For Paul goes right on to say, "Therefore . . ." (chapter 12, verse 1):

> Therefore [because God is like this and you are like that], I urge you, brothers, in view of God's mercy, to offer yourselves as living sacrifices, holy and pleasing to God—which is your spiritual worship.

I don't like "spiritual worship" as a translation of the Greek here; literally, it is "logical service." It is only reasonable for man to be available to God. It is the logical reason for your existence. "Therefore," he says, "bring your bodies." If you are Christians, your spirits have already been surrendered to God. But you are trying to live split lives, schizophrenic lives, if your body does not follow what your spirit has already done. Now put your body where your mouth is and follow through with what your spirit has said to God. Be his available instrument.

What Paul is describing here is not an act of the moment —it is a commitment for the rest of your life. You are going to make your body available to God for as long as you live. Paul does not talk about your soul or your spirit because you never can do anything without your body in this life. So put your body on the line. Bring it, a living sacrifice, and the God of greatness and glory, of infinite riches and wisdom and power, will fill that body with his own amazing life, and you will never find life to be the same again.

7

Living Day by Day

We are going to take a closer look now at the opening verse of Romans 12, which is, as I have already stressed, the conclusion of Paul's argument in chapter 11. Paul says, because God is like this—rich and wise and great and glorious, a God of love and mercy, and you are like this—ignorant of the future, forgetful of the past, unable to control the present. . . .

> Therefore, I urge you, brothers, in view of God's mercy, to offer yourselves as living sacrifices, holy and pleasing to God— which is your spiritual worship. Do not conform any longer to the pattern of this world, but be transformed by the renewing of your mind. Then you will be able to test and approve what God's will is—his good, pleasing and perfect will (vv. 1,2).

These are familiar words. I know you have read them many times. I like the way the Jerusalem Bible translates the first sentence:

> Think of God's mercies, my brothers, and worship him, I beg you, in a way that is worthy—by offering him your living bodies.

That is what we sing in the closing words of that great hymn, "When I Survey the Wondrous Cross":

> Love so amazing, so divine,
> Demands my soul, my life, my all.

When Paul says to "present your bodies," he uses the Greek aorist tense. That means it is something you do once for all; it is not something you do over and over again. You do it once, and then you live the rest of your life on that basis. There comes a time in a Christian's life when God wants you to bring your body to him, recognizing for the rest of your life his right to use your body for his purposes.

Source of the Trouble

It amazes me that God would ever want our bodies. You may ask, why would he want my body? I can hardly stand it myself, at times. But God says, "Bring your body." Perhaps the most striking thing is that Paul has been talking about the body all the way through this section of Romans. In fact, he tells us the body is the seat of what he calls "the flesh," the antagonistic nature within us that does not like what God likes and does not want to do what God wants. We all have it, and somehow it is located in or connected with the body. Our body is the source of temptation. It is what grows weak and wobbly. That God would want this body is unbelievable, and yet he does.

Some of us, I know, feel like saying, "Lord, surely you don't want this body! Let me tell you something about it! It's got B.O.! It snores! It has a bad heart, Lord. It has a dirty mind. You don't want this body. I have trouble with this body. It is always tripping me up. My spirit is great, and I worship you with my soul—but the body, Lord, that's what gets me down!" But the Lord says, "Bring your body. Let me tell you something about it. I know all about it. I know more about it than you do. I know all the things you tell me about it plus some things you haven't learned yet.

Let me tell you something. By means of the blood of Jesus, and by the work of the Holy Spirit, I have made it (what does Paul say?) 'holy and pleasing' to God."

That is the beautiful appeal of this verse. It is not telling us we have to get all cleaned up and get our lives straightened out in every way and become perfect before we can offer ourselves to God. Paul's word is, "I urge you, brothers and sisters, in view of God's mercy, to offer yourselves as living sacrifices. Bring your bodies (that is what it says in the Greek—"your bodies," not "yourselves") as a living sacrifice unto God." Bring your body with all its problems, with all the difficulty you have with it, with all the temptations—bring it just the way it is! I don't know how that affects you, but it encourages me greatly. All the other religions in the world tell us that somehow we have to clean up our lives first, and then offer them to God. God never talks that way. He says, "You come to me just the way you are. I am the answer to your problems; therefore, you must start with me. You can't handle those problems yourself. Don't start with the idea that you have to get them straightened out. Come to me, because I have the answers."

Week-long Worship

Furthermore, Paul tells us, this is the only thing that makes sense. "This is your logical worship." This is the way you worship God. I hear many people talking about worship these days. When you come to a church you come to worship corporately, together. But worship does not start or end in church. You are worshiping or you are not worshiping all week long, depending on what you do with your body. Is it his? Is it his to use right where you are—at your work, in your home, with your family? Worship is allowing God to use your body and to be the dynamic that works through that body in every situation. God says that is your logical worship. That is the only thing that makes sense.

God says if *you* use your body, you will misuse it, abuse it. You will use it for things the body was never intended to be used for. Or you will use it in such a way that it will be destroyed or hurt. We know this is true. But if you give your body to God, he says he will use it rightly. You will either ruin it, if you use it yourself, or you will spend so much time preserving it, painting it, pouring lotions on it, exposing it to the sun, and all the other things we do, that you will never get around to using it for what God has intended. "So bring it to me," God says, "and I will use it wherever you go, and I will use it in such a way as to bring peace and to give joy and to heal hurt and show love and healing and grace wherever you are. I will bless the world through your body."

Therefore, the only logical, sensible thing to do with your body is to bring it to the Lord and say, "Lord, here it is, just as it is, without any attempt to improve it or make it better. Take me, Lord, and begin to use me." Well, that sounds great, doesn't it? You ask, "Okay, Lord, but how do I do this? How does it work?" The Lord says, "Once you bring your body to me, I will take it. But then there are two things that you need to keep doing. First, 'Do not conform any longer to the pattern of this world.' Second, 'Be transformed by the renewing of your mind.' Then you will be able to test and approve what God's will is—his good, pleasing, and perfect will." These two commands are both in the present tense. That means they are things that you keep on doing. You bring your body once—you give it to God and you base the rest of your life on that commitment—then you go out and do these two things every day.

Sell Your TV

First, "Do not be conformed to the pattern of this world." Literally, this means "the schemes of this world," the schemes that men come up with, by which they regulate and run their lives. The word of the Lord is, "Stop being conformed to that." "Oh," you say, "I know exactly what you are talking about. That means you should not smoke or drink or play cards or, if you are really, really spiritual, you

sell your television set and never drink coffee or tea again."
You say that is being spiritual and not being conformed to
the world.

I grew up thinking that way, and there was always a particular list of forbidden activities for me to avoid. Many
other things the world did were not on the list, but the
things mentioned above were always on it. I had to learn,
through rather painful experience, that those things are
neither good nor bad in themselves. I know people who have
given up all of them, and yet they are still saturated by the
spirit of the age. That is what this word really means; be
not conformed to the pattern of this age, the spirit of the
age, the philosophy of life that surrounds us on every side.

The spirit of the age, you see, is always the same. It never
changes from generation to generation. The basis of it is
clearly the advancement of self. Everyone in the world lives
to advance himself. "What do I get out of this? What's in
it for me?" What this word is saying to us is, "Don't be stuck
in that kind of thinking, because that is what brings heart-
ache and ruin and disaster into our lives. Don't live on that
basis anymore. Don't get caught up with that kind of thinking; it's wrong! It is an approach to life that is twisted and
distorted, and it won't work. Don't be trapped by it."

What is the spirit of this age? It is to seek my personal
happiness. If the advancement of self is the basis for all life,
then the goal of all life is my happiness. You hear that on
every side. Unfortunately it has infiltrated the church as
well. Christians talk this way just as much as anyone else.
They say, "The reason I am working and living is to have
my needs met, my desires fulfilled." I hear people talking
about church this way: "I'm thinking of leaving this church
and going to another one." If you ask them why they'll
reply, "Because this one doesn't meet my needs," as though
the only reason for ever going to church is to have your needs
met! That is the thinking of the world, the spirit of the age.
To be conformed to that way of thinking is to be conformed
to the world, regardless of whether you drink or smoke or
chew or play cards.

Then there are the methods of the world. You only have to look around to see what those are: rivalry and competition, getting ahead of the other guy, grabbing what's mine before someone else gets it, hanging onto everything I've got no matter what it costs in terms of hurt or pain to someone else. The apostle is saying, "Don't let the world around you pressure you into thinking that way any longer." The pressure to conform pervades all society. All around us a whole climate of life is pressuring us, squeezing us, insisting we conform, making it costly to us if we don't.

Response to Stardom

I heard recently of an incident in the life of Jerome Hines, the Metropolitan Opera singer. As a boy growing up in California, he became convinced that he had a good voice. Someone urged him to seek training for it, and so he did. He became possessed with a desire to become a star in the Metropolitan Opera Company. That was what he lived for. He gave up all other activities, all other pursuits, all other pleasures, to give himself to the necessary work of training to become an opera star. Perfecting the arts of intonation, of musical projection, he learned several languages so he could sing operatic roles. He gave himself totally to that tremendous desire within him to be a star in the Metropolitan Opera. Finally it came true. He became a star. And he said it was empty, hollow. One day he heard a man singing. The voice was as good as his, and the man could have done what he did. He heard Beverly Shea singing, "I'd Rather Have Jesus." The words he sang were,

> I'd rather have Jesus than silver or gold.
> I'd rather be His than have riches untold.
> I'd rather have Jesus than houses or land.
> I'd rather be led by His nail-pierced hands
> Than to be the king of a vast domain,
> And be held in sin's dread sway.
> I'd rather have Jesus than anything
> This world affords today.

That song got to Jerome Hines. He began to think about it and, out of that incident, he became a Christian. But he didn't quit the opera. Many people thought he should have. They thought the opera was "worldly." No, opera is not worldly—except to those who think like worldlings and live like worldlings in the opera. Jerome Hines stayed in opera, but everything was different. He was no longer singing for the advancement of Jerome Hines, he was singing for the glory of God. He dedicated his art, his work, his all to that purpose. God does not take us out of the world; he wants us to live in it, but to change our thinking.

A few years ago Hines had an opportunity to sing the role that he had always wanted to sing. He had trained for it through months and months of hard work, and he was given the role. His contract stated that he was to sing that role in the opera for ten years. When he went to the opera house to practice, he found some people performing a rather lewd dance. He asked, "What is this?" He was told, "This is the choreography that introduces the opera." He said, "There's nothing in the opera like this!" "No," they said, "we're changing it a bit, modernizing it, bringing it up to date." Jerome Hines said, "I won't sing if you are going to have this kind of dance in it." He was told he had better go talk to Mr. Bing.

Jerome Hines went to Rudolph Bing, general manager of the Metropolitan Opera, and said to him, "Sir, if you have that dance in the opera I am not going to sing in it." Bing told him, "If you don't sing, you will be ostracized and blacklisted in opera. You are under contract to sing." Hines said, "Sir, I can't sing in that opera. I am not going to let my name be used to entice people to come in to see filth like this. You can break me, sir, and the union can break me. I've worked hard for months to train for this role, but I will not sing in your opera if that dance is in it." Bing said, "Jerome, you don't have to sing. If you really feel that way, you don't have to sing; we'll get someone else. But we can't change the contract."

So Jerome Hines had to give up that role. It cost him, over

the period of ten years, something like a hundred thousand dollars. How many of us are willing to give our bodies to God in such a way that we would be willing to give up a hundred thousand dollars rather than do something that would be offensive to the Lord? This is what Paul means by not being conformed to this world—not going along with its pattern of thinking, not being willing to go in for all it goes in for in its pursuit of pleasure and happiness. "That's tough," you say. You bet it's tough! If you do that day after day it gets very hard, because you are under constant pressure—and it gets to you after a while. Everyone is thinking this way, everyone wants to do that, no one understands you—so why don't you give in?

Thinking with the Mind of Christ

There is only one answer to that question. To stand up against that kind of pressure you need what Paul talks about next: "but be transformed by the renewing of your mind." There is no way you can keep from being conformed to the world unless you are being transformed by the renewing of your mind. Something has to happen to your thinking. You can't go on thinking the way the world around you thinks and not give in and be conformed to what it does. What we need is a change of thinking. That comes day by day by being renewed again and again and again. You need a mind that will see through all these silly schemes of the world. In the Scriptures that kind of mind is called "the mind of Christ." The mind of Christ is to look at life as Jesus does, seeing life as he sees it. It is seeing what is really there and not what seems to be there, seeing what really is important, not what appears to be important. You can't have that mind unless your mind is being renewed every day.

The mind of Christ does not say that the basis of life is the advancement of self. When it looks at the world it says that the basis for living, the reason for life, is to serve God and to advance his will. Not your will, but his will be done;

not the building of your kingdom and your empire, but the advancement of his kingdom. This is really what human beings are here for, and to maintain that kind of thinking in the midst of the world takes a renewed mind.

I was conversing with a young businessman one day. He told me that he had made a list of all the reasons why he is working at his company: the advantages it gave him, the salary, the prestige and status, the opportunity to rub shoulders with men in his profession who could help him, the opportunity to be involved in work in which he found intense pleasure.

Then, when he finished the list, he looked at it and said to himself, "That's just a human list—the things that just anybody would put down. I'm a Christian. I ought to have other reasons than these for being here." So he took another piece of paper and sat down and began to list all the reasons why God wanted him there. He began to see things he hadn't seen before. For one thing he saw that God had him there because the fellow at the next desk needed his help. Then, too, he had an opportunity to bring a witness to his whole organization that wouldn't be there otherwise. There were occasions when he could help people with their problems and give them Christian insights to aid in their personal and emotional needs. When he finished, he began to realize that these were the real reasons why he was in that job. How much money he made and his advancement were really quite trivial; the enduring thing, the thing that would last forever, was not what he got out of it, but what God got out of it.

That is what this passage is talking about—renewing your mind so that you see life the way God sees it. The mind of Christ sees that the goal of living is not to please yourself but to please God. And the way you please God is to depend on him, to expect him to work through you, where you are; to believe that he has the power and the wisdom and the strength to somehow, in the situation in which you find yourself, do things in ways that you can't anticipate or even dream of. God is pleased when people venture out in faith.

Settlers and Pioneers

I recently found a paper by a man named Wes Seeliger describing the two kinds of theology there are in Christian life today. It was put in terms of the Old West. One was called "Settler Theology," and the other, "Pioneer Theology." In Settler Theology the church is the courthouse in a little town; it is in charge of everything. In Pioneer Theology the church is a covered wagon, out on the trail, never stopping, involved in battles and bearing the scars of many fights, getting stuck in the mud and being pulled out again.

In Settler Theology God is the mayor. He lives up on the top floor of the courthouse and keeps an eagle eye on everything going on in town. In Pioneer Theology God is the trail boss, rough and rugged and tough and hard-hitting; he won't let anyone stop—he keeps them going down the trail. He gets down, shoulder to the wheel, when they get stuck in the mud.

In Settler Theology Jesus is the sheriff. He wears a white hat and goes around plugging all the bad boys who come into town. He determines who goes to jail or who doesn't. In Pioneer Theology Jesus is the scout, out ahead of the party, telling where the wagon is to go next, exposed to all the dangers of the trail. He is the pioneer's pioneer.

In Settler Theology the Holy Spirit is the saloon girl. She keeps everyone comforted and happy. In Pioneer Theology, the Holy Spirit is the buffalo hunter who provides the daily meat for the wagon train. He amuses himself by going up to the courthouse window every Sunday, when all the settlers are having an ice cream party, and firing off a tremendous blast from his shotgun, scaring the living daylights out of all the people inside.

In Settler Theology the preacher is the banker. He keeps all the resources in town under control. Everything has to go through him. In Pioneer Theology the preacher is the cook. He just dishes out the food that the buffalo hunter provides. He's no better than any of the other pioneers, he just keeps them fed.

This paper is a tremendous overview of New Testament Christianity. Christians are not sent into the world to build their own little nests, to feather them up and keep them nice and comfortable and to try to get by without being polluted by the things around them. Jesus said that we are to go into the world like sheep in the midst of wolves. We are exposed to danger and pressure and trouble and battle all the time. The only thing that will keep us from succumbing to this subversive propaganda to which we are constantly exposed is that we constantly have our minds renewed by the Word of God.

In Line with God's Word

How do you get your mind renewed? Well, one place it happens is at church, wherever there is an exposition of the Scriptures, so that we hear once again what the truth is— not what everyone around is telling us is true. Your mind is also renewed in your personal Bible study, when you sit down with the Word of God. When you are confused and don't know where you are, you renew your mind by reading through a passage and thinking it through and letting the Word speak to your heart. Then you go back to your routine and determine that your life will be in line with the Word of God. Your mind is renewed in prayer and by spiritual fellowship with other believers. These are all part of the process of having a renewed mind.

Now, what are you going to do with your life? Are you going to wrap it up in a napkin of affluence and bury it in forty years of self-indulgence? That would be the dullest experience you could have. When you come before the throne of God, you will find out that you have simply wasted all those years. Oh, you will be there, if you know the Lord, but you will find you have wasted your life, and it will be worth little before his throne.

But you are to be willing to bring your body to God and say, "Lord, here it is. I have trouble with it, and I'm sure you will, too, but here it is. You wanted it. I give it to you for the rest of my life, to be your instrument for whatever you want." Then God says, "All right, I'll take it." If you come on that basis, beginning to recognize the systematic brainwashing of the world and refusing it, and constantly renewing your thinking in the truth as it is found in Jesus and the Word of God, then I will tell you something: You are going to have an exciting life, beyond anything you ever dreamed. It will never be dull. It will be terribly difficult sometimes, but never dull, never boring.

Many years ago a friend of mine was walking through Union Station in Chicago. It was busy and crowded. He had been thinking of what we might do with his life. It suddenly dawned on him that the only logical thing he could do with his life, since it belonged to God and had been redeemed by the Lord, was to give it to him and ask him to use it. Right in the midst of the crowd he stopped and drew a little mark with his toe. Then he stood on that mark and said, "Lord, here I am, I am yours. The rest of my life, whatever you want me to do, if you will show me and convince me that is what you want, I will do it. The attitudes you want me to have, I will have. As I study and read your Word, I will try to carry out what you tell me to do, and think the way you tell me to think. Here I am, Lord; you do with my life as you want." That commitment service, held in Union Station in Chicago, was known only by this man and God. But God picked that man up and began to use him in remarkable ways. He has traveled the world and touched hundreds of lives because God used him.

If you want to stand where you are now and draw a little mark on the floor with your toe, that's fine. Give yourself to God, if that is what you want. He doesn't make anyone do this. That is why Paul puts it in these terms: "I beseech you, brothers, I beg you. It is the logical outcome of your life, the only thing that makes sense." But will you give yourself to him, so you can never forget that you did it right here and right now? Every time you come back to this spot you will think about it. "This is where I gave myself to God. This is where I said he had a right to use me. He can use my body and all that I am for the rest of my life."

8

Who Am I, Lord?

Be transformed by having your mind renewed! This is what Paul tells us. From verse 3 through the rest of chapter 12 the apostle Paul explains specifically what it means to have your thinking changed.

The place to start is with yourself. That is always where God starts. He never wants to change others until he has changed you. Jesus said, *"First* remove the beam that is in your own eye, then you will see clearly how to help your brother remove the little sliver that is in his eye." The order of this is so important! In verses 3 through 8 the apostle tells us two things about thinking of ourselves. First, what to think about who we are; and then what to think about the gifts God has given us. Let's begin with the word about our view of ourselves:

> For by the grace given to me I say to every one of you: Do not think of yourself more highly than you ought, but rather think of yourself with sober judgment, in accordance with the measure of faith God has given you (v. 3).

Paul is saying, first, to think about yourself. Many people get the idea that the Christian life consists of never thinking about yourself. Because we know that ultimately we are to reach out to others, we think there is never any place for

thinking about ourselves. That is wrong. Some Christians
have abused this to such a degree that all they think about
is themselves, and they are forever going around taking
their spiritual temperature and feeling their spiritual pulse.

It is true the Scriptures tell you to examine yourself, to
see whether you are in the faith or not; "to see whether
Christ be in you," as Paul writes to the Corinthians. But it
is wrong to think continually of nothing but yourself. Nevertheless, it is quite right to take time, occasionally, to evaluate yourself and where you are in your Christian life and
experience. In fact, the apostle exhorts us with his apostolic
authority to do so. "For by the grace given to me"—that is,
the gift of apostleship—on the basis of that office he exhorts
every one of us to take time to think through where we are
and what is going on in our lives.

Avoid Overrating

But Paul stresses that you have to do this in a way that
avoids overrating yourself. "Do not think of yourself more
highly than you ought." I am sure he puts this first because
it is such a natural tendency with us. Our flesh, our inherited
Adamic nature, loves to think about itself, and to think of
itself very highly. I am sure you have had the experience of
realizing, all of a sudden, that your view of yourself is usually much higher than other people's view of you. That is
why we get upset with people—because they don't agree
with our opinion about ourselves.

There are two ways that people express an exalted self-
view. We are familiar with the loud-mouthed braggart who
goes around taking every occasion he can to tell you how
smart he is, how much he's done, how capable he is, how
much he can do if you just give him a chance. But there are
some who realize that people don't like braggarts, so they
revert to the opposite form of the same problem, which is
to deplore themselves, to talk about themselves as though
they are nothing or no one. But that is merely another form
of pride.

The reason you do this (I know, because I've done it myself) is that you hope others will correct you. You tell them all these bad things about yourself with the expectation that people will say, "No, no, you're not like that at all!" And you say, "Come on, keep it up. Tell me more! Talk me out of this!" Of course, the way to make the true motive clear with people who do this is simply to agree with them. If you hear someone talking like that, just say, "Well, I have to admit you are right," and watch the reaction. He'll be very upset with you, because you have really offended his pride. It is a dissembling, a pretense to humility. Paul says to avoid either one of these approaches.

But there is a proper way to think about yourself, and that is to observe the limits God has given "Do not think . . . more highly than you ought (to think)." There is an "oughtness" to this matter of thinking about yourself. What is this "oughtness"? Negatively, the Scriptures suggest we ought not to judge ourselves by paying attention to our feelings. I am amazed at how many people determine what they are like or are able to do by the way they happen to feel at the moment. They trust their feelings, as though feelings give adequate and trustworthy information about themselves. But feelings can change and fluctuate a hundred times a minute. They are dependent upon many factors over which we have no control, such as whether our glands are working properly, or whether the sun is shining, or whether we ate too much at a previous meal, or whether we got enough sleep the night before—all these factors affect our feelings. Therefore the most foolish thing in the world is to judge yourself on the basis of how you feel at any given moment.

Now, feelings are important, and I don't mean to rule them out entirely. Sometimes people get the idea that feelings are all wrong. No, feelings are not wrong; they just should not be the basis for your evaluation of yourself.

On what basis, then, should you evaluate yourself? The answer, of course, is on how God sees you. That is reality— what God says you are. That is the realistic way to think about yourself. It is a twofold evaluation, as the apostle makes clear in this verse.

Something to Watch

First of all, he says, Do not think of yourself more highly than you ought, "but think of yourself with sober judgment." So, *first,* think soberly about yourself. What does this mean? What will sober you? Well, surely that refers to the teaching of the Scriptures on the Fall. We are all fallen creatures. All of us have within us this Adamic nature which is not to be trusted at all. And as long as we are in the flesh, in the body, we are going to have this nature. Therefore, the first thing to remember about yourself is that there is something you have to watch. There will be something within you that you can't ever trust. There will be thoughts and attitudes and temptations in your life which are distorted and wrong. And they will always be there. Therefore, first of all, think soberly about yourself.

Second, think "with the measure of faith that God has given you." That is, look back over all God has told you about what has happened since you have come to Christ. The degree to which you accept what God has said about you will give you confidence and courage and ability to function as a human being any day, or at any given task. You have that courage and ability according to how much you believe what God has said.

And what has God said about you? Look back over all the tremendous truth given in the first eight chapters of Romans: We are no longer in Adam, in our spirit, but are now tied to Christ. He lives with us, his power is available to us. The Holy Spirit has come to enable us to say no to all the evil forces and temptations that we come up against, so that sin shall not have dominion over us, for we are not under the law but under grace. That is the way to think about yourself. Remember that you are always going to have to be on guard because of the evil of the flesh within you, but you can always win because of the grace of God

and the righteousness of Jesus Christ and the gift of the
Holy Spirit which you have.

When I get up in the morning I try to remind myself of
three things: *First*, I am made in the image of God. I am
not an animal and I don't have to behave like an animal,
because I have an ability within me, given to me by God
himself, the ability to react and relate to God. Therefore
I can behave as a man and not as a beast. *Second*, I am
filled with the Spirit of God. The most amazing thing has
happened! Though I didn't deserve it in the least degree,
I have the power of God at work within me. I have become,
in some sense, the bearer of God, and God himself is willing
to be at work in me in terms of the little problems and the
little pressures that I am going to go through this day. *Third*,
I remind myself that I am part of the plan of God, that
God is working out all things to a great and final purpose in
the earth, and I am part of it. What I do today has purpose
and significance and meaning. It is not just a meaningless
thing that I am going to go through. Even the smallest incident, the most apparently insignificant word or relationship is involved in that great plan. Therefore all has meaning
and purpose.

That gives me confidence without conceit. I have a sense
of being able to cope, of being able to handle life. I know
I don't deserve this gift of worth and grace, and yet I have
it. Therefore I can't be conceited about it, but I can be confident in it. I don't know anything else that can set you on
your feet like that.

In Front of the Mirror

Now Paul moves to our life in the church and he takes
up the subject of the gifts that God has given. Not only are
you who you are because of the work of Christ, but you
also have what you have because of his work. Here the
apostle says,

> Just as each of us has one body with many members, and these
> members do not all have the same function, so in Christ we

who are many form one body, and each member belongs to all the others (v. 4).

That is a beautiful picture of the church. I don't know what you think about the church. We have grown up with various backgrounds and experiences in churches, and I am sure all of us have a mental picture of what the church ought to be. But here is where we need our thinking changed. We need to be renewed in our minds. God has told us that his church is like a human body. If you want a good course in ecclesiology, just stand in front of your mirror some morning without your clothes on and examine your body. That is what the church is like.

The *first* thing that will impress you is that there is only one body there, not two. So there is only one church in all the world. All Christians belong to it, and it doesn't make any difference whether they have a denominational label or not. If they have been born of the Spirit of God they are members of that church, and there is only one church. Therefore, wherever the members meet one another, they already belong to each other. Whether you have your name on a church roll somewhere is of no significance whatsoever. There is only one church, one body.

The *second* thing that will strike you as you look at your own body is that it has members. It isn't just a trunk, but it has arms, legs, feet, toes, fingers, eyes, ears, and a number of other interesting protuberances. And they are all for a purpose. They are part of the body; they belong to the body. So also, the church of Christ has many members, and they are different from one another. That is what I like about the church—the diversity of its members. Yet that is so contrary to the spirit of the age. In this age, the spirit of the world around us is one of uniformity. Everyone is pressured to look, act, talk, and think alike. Join a club and you have to dress as they dress, drive the same general class of car, and so on. Join another club and you have to change your way of speaking. I don't know why we have this mentality that forces us to duplicate everything. Even in the church people want to turn out Christians like so many sausages—all alike.

But that is not God's idea of the church. His idea is to have diversity within the church. There are many members, and they are not to be alike. That is the joy of it. They don't come from the same class or the same race; they are not the same color, and they don't even have the same gifts. They have many gifts. A true church is one where people are beginning to recognize that diversity and rejoice in it.

And yet, Paul says, though these members do not all have the same function, each one belongs to all the others. That is unique. No other organization in the world can say that about itself. In all other organizations the members are individually there for what each can get out of it. But in the church of Jesus Christ, we belong to one another. We share with one another. Paul says we are to have the same care, one for another. Isn't this remarkable! How terrible it would be if all Christians were exactly the same.

Years ago, when Ron Ritchie was our high school pastor, he was teaching 1 Corinthians 12 to some of the kids. To illustrate his point he painted a football like one huge eye, a human eye, with a big, round pupil. He wrapped it in a blanket and put it under his arm and showed it to the kids. "What do you think of my baby?" he asked. They would look at it and say, "Oh, gross!" Here was this eye staring out at them. He asked them, "What if your girlfriend was just an eye? If you took her out on a date there would be this great big eye sitting across from you in the booth. What a date that would be!" He drove home this point very forcibly: We are not just one member; we are many. All the body is not an eye. Yet, we are to have the same care one for another. Even though we are different, we are to love each other because we belong to each other. We share the same life together.

That is why you are to get along with other Christians—not because we like them, necessarily, or that they are very nice, but just because we belong to each other. They are your brothers and sisters. And when they hurt you will hurt, whether you know it or not. And when they are honored, you will be honored, whether you know it or not.

A number of years ago I fell and injured my wrist rather severely. It swelled up and became very painful. And the rest of my body felt so bad about it that it sat up all night to keep it company. That is what the body of Christ is to do when one member is hurt. We are tied to one another, and when one hurts, all hurt.

Graceful Functions

Not only is that true, but Paul goes on to point out that we have gifts that determine our function within the body:

> We have different gifts, according to the grace given us. If a man's gift is prophesying, let him use it in proportion to his faith. If it is serving, let him serve; if it is teaching, let him teach; if it is encouraging, let him encourage; if it is contributing to the needs of others, let him give generously; if it is leadership, let him govern diligently; if it is showing mercy, let him do it cheerfully (v. 6).

That is only a sampling of gifts. Many others are mentioned in 1 Corinthians 12, 1 Peter 4, and Ephesians 4. You have to put them all together to get the total list of gifts available to us. But the point the apostle makes is this: God has given gifts. Paul calls them "graces," and we have different gifts, according to the specific gift of grace that is given to us. I like that term for gifts because it indicates something about them. Graces are graceful. Something that is graceful is a delight to watch, and this is true about a spiritual gift. A gift is an ability God has given you because he wants you to function along this line. It enables you to do this thing so naturally, smoothly, and beautifully that others will take note of it and ask you to do it and enjoy watching you do it. You will enjoy it, too. When you are using your spiritual gift you are fulfilled. It is called a "grace" because it is not a difficult, painful thing to do; it is something you delight in doing. And you can improve in it as you do it. Therefore it is one of the things that will make life interesting and fulfilling for you.

Imagine how hurt you would be if you prepared gifts for your children, wrapped them all up in beautiful packages and put them under the Christmas tree, and then handed them out to your children and they just took the gifts and laid them aside. What if they said, "Thank you," and never bothered to open the packages? Can you imagine how the Lord must feel, having given us gifts to use, when we never take the trouble to find out what they are, and never put them to work, excusing ourselves by saying that we can't do anything? The Word of God tells us that not a single Christian is left out in this distribution of gifts. It is clear from this account that the gifts Paul lists here are intended to be used.

The first gift mentioned is prophesying. In 1 Corinthians 12 and 14 Paul tells us this is one of the best gifts of all. This is the gift you ought to desire earnestly to be shown in your midst, because basically it is the gift of expounding Scripture, making Scripture come alive. It comes from a root word in Greek that means "to cause to shine," and it refers to the ability to take the Word of God and make it shine. Thus everyone sees what to do and where to go and how to act and function. Peter says, "We have a more sure word of prophecy that shines as a light in a dark place." John Calvin describes prophecy as "the peculiar gift of explaining revelation." Paul says if you have the gift, use it. It is not just for people who go to seminary; there may be many in a congregation who will have the gift of prophesying. Then use it. But you must use it according to the proportion of your faith. That is, stay with what you know. Don't try to get into areas that you don't yet understand. That will come later as you grow in the use of your gift. Start where you do understand Scripture, make it clear to people, explain it. That is the gift of prophesying.

There are some who have the gift of serving. This is a beautiful and common gift. Many people have it. I believe it is the same gift which is called "the gift of helps" in 1

Corinthians 12. It is the word from which we get our word
"deacon." It is "to deaconize," i.e., to serve as an usher, to
do banking on behalf of the church, or caring for widows,
or serving on committees. Serving is the ability to help people with such a cheerful spirit that they are blessed by it.
All of us know people like that. We just love to have them
around because they are so eager to serve and they do it
so willingly and cheerfully that everyone is helped and
blessed by them. What a tremendous gift that is!

Find an Occasion

"If [his gift] is teaching, let him teach." Teaching is the
ability to impart knowledge and information, to instruct the
mind. Prophesying goes much deeper. It instructs the heart
and moves the will. But teaching instructs the mind and is
the basis for understanding many of the truths of Scriptures.
Therefore the gift of teaching is a great gift, and widely
distributed in the body. I suspect that at least 30 percent
or more of any Christian group would have the gift of teaching. If you have it, don't wait for someone to ask you to
teach. The church didn't give you these gifts. The pastor
didn't give you these gifts. God gave them to you—your
responsibility is to put them to work. Don't wait for someone to invite you to exercise your gift. That may happen,
and be glad if it does, but you still have the responsibility
to use the gift God has given you, whether anyone asks you
to or not. You find the occasion. Find someone who doesn't
know as much as you know and teach him, if you have the
gift of teaching.

Then there is the gift of encouragement. That was the gift
that Barnabas had. He was called "the son of encouragement," which is what the name Barnabas means. His name
was Joseph, but no one called him Joe; they called him
Barney. In the stories of Barnabas in the Scriptures he is
always found with his arm around someone's shoulder, encouraging him, comforting him, urging him on. This is a
marvelous gift in the church. If you have the gift of en-

couragement, start anywhere and use it. God gave it to you, therefore use that gift.

Then there is the gift of giving, contributing. Did you know that was a gift? That means God will give you something to give, and then he will give you a desire to give it. If you have that gift, use it! The more you use it, the more you will have to give. It is part of the way you function in the body of Christ, and many can use that gift. Paul says, "Let him give generously." That is not quite an accurate translation. What Paul is really saying is, "Let him give with simplicity." It means without ostentation, without calling people's attention to it. I heard of a man who stood up in a meeting and said, "I want to give $100—anonymously." You can't give that way if you have the gift of giving; you give with simplicity, without making a big deal out of it. Just give the gift as unto God and delight in the opportunity to be used by the hand of God.

Then the gift of leadership is mentioned. Specifically, that word means "leading meetings." It comes from a root which means "to stand up before others." If you have that gift, there are all kinds of meetings waiting to be led. But when you use it, Paul says, do it with diligence. That is, don't wing it. Do it thoughtfully; think it through in advance. Make yourself ready for it and use the meeting to its fullest purpose. The gift of leadership is a great gift.

Then, finally, Paul mentions the gift of showing mercy. I delight in some of the people of our church who have the gift of showing mercy. There is young girl who comes and brings retarded children, sits with them in her lap, and interprets the service to them. There is another young girl who brings a dear old lady who is partially crippled and nearly blind. The girl brings her almost every Sunday and ministers to her. Mercy, you see, is helping those who are undeserving and neglected by others. The gift of showing mercy is a marvelous gift within the church, and many have it. If you have it, don't wait for someone to show you what to do—start doing it.

Sometimes great and marvelous organizations have grown

up out of a single person beginning to exercise his gift. A ministry for physically and mentally handicapped children, called "Green Pastures," has grown up out of the exercise of the gift of mercy by a single individual. There is another ministry reaching out to the vast crowd of homosexuals in our area. It was organized by someone who had a vision, a gift of showing mercy—someone who had an understanding of the homosexual's need and a desire to help. These people are starting out alone, but others will join them.

Speaking or Serving

There are many other gifts not mentioned here, as I said. But no matter where you find a list of gifts, there are always two divisions. Peter gives this division to us in 1 Peter 4:10,11. He says, "Each one should use whatever spiritual gift he has received to serve others, faithfully administering God's grace in its various forms. If anyone speaks, he should do it as one speaking the very words of God. If anyone serves, he should do it with the strength God provides, so that in all things God may be praised through Jesus Christ." There are the two divisions, speaking and serving. In Romans 12 the first four gifts listed have to do with speaking; the last three have to do with serving. There are two basic functions, then, of every believer in the body of Christ. Either you speak, or you serve—one or the other. And everyone is to be involved. Dr. F. B. Meyer, a great Bible teacher of the last generation, said this about the local church:

> It is urgently needful that the Christian people of our charge should come to understand that they are not a company of invalids, to be wheeled about, or fed by hand, cosseted, nursed, and comforted, the minister being the Head Physician and Nurse; but a garrison in an enemy's country, every soul of which should have some post of duty, at which he should be prepared to make any sacrifice rather than quitting.

Now that, I think, is a biblical picture of the church, a church functioning as God intended it to function.

Now we come to this question: Who are you, anyway? Every morning you ought to ask yourself that. Who am I? Your answer should come from the Scriptures: I am a son of God among the sons of men. I am equipped with the power of God to labor today. In the very work that is given to me today God will be with me, doing it through me. I am gifted with special abilities to help people in various areas, and I don't have to wait until Sunday to start to utilize these gifts. I can do it at my work, I can do it anywhere. I can exercise the gift that God has given me as soon as I begin to find out what it is, by taking note of my desires and by asking others what they see in me and by trying out various things. I am going to set myself to the lifelong task of keeping that gift busy.

Paul had to write to Timothy and say, "Stir up the gift that is in you, that which was given you by the Holy Spirit." Perhaps Timothy was letting it slide. But we are expected to stir it up. I hope you present your bodies afresh today, so you can find that gift and put it to work. Be busy doing what God has sent you here to do. Perhaps you want to renew again your request to God to help you in the search for your spiritual gift and to lead you to put it to work, with a view toward the day when you stand before him and he asks, "What did you do with the gift that I gave you?"

9

How to Hug

The title of this chapter, "How to Hug," was suggested to me by a story I once heard. A man was walking down the street, and as he passed a used book store he saw a book in the window with this title, "How to Hug." Being of a somewhat romantic nature, he went in to buy the book. To his chagrin, he discovered that it was a certain volume of an encyclopedia and covered the subjects "How" to "Hug."

I have often thought of the church as like that. Everyone knows that the church is a place where love ought to be manifested, and many people have come to church hoping to find a demonstration of love, only to discover an encyclopedia on theology. But I am grateful that God is changing this situation today. Thank God that hugs are returning to the churches. In the early church the Christians actually greeted one another with a holy kiss. You don't see that too often these days, but perhaps it is coming back.

Love without Wax

In Romans 12:9–21, you can see that the theme is clearly given in the very first sentence: "Love must be sincere." Our English word "sincere" comes from the Latin *sincerus*—

without wax. The word literally reflects what the Greek says here, "Let love be without hypocrisy." The Revised Standard Version translates it, "Let love be genuine." Phillips says, "Let us have no imitation Christian love."

The primary character of the early Christian community was this: it was a place where love was demonstrated—so much so that people began to imitate it. Every writer in the New Testament stresses the need for love. In 1 Timothy 1:5, Paul writes to his young son in the faith and says, "The end of our endeavor is love." That is where it all comes out. "The end of our endeavor is love, out of a pure heart, a good conscience and a sincere faith." Peter says, "Above all, love each other deeply . . ." (1 Peter 4:8). Paul reminds us here and in other places that this love must be a genuine love, not phony, not hypocritical.

In those early days of the church it was easy to imitate love if you didn't really have it. People fell into the habit, as they do today, of pretending they loved, using loving terms and gestures, but really not feeling it in their hearts. This, of course, is hypocrisy, and this is what this passage in Romans warns against. Don't let your love be hypocritical, don't put it on. We are living in an age in which this is the very spirit of the times—to project an image, to pretend one is something he is not. All the world holds that up before us; through the media of television and radio we are actually encouraged to be something we are not. No one seems to see how phony this is. But in the church it is intolerable. That we should be in any sense phony in our love is a violation of all the Lord came to do. Sham love, of course, comes from the flesh, that pretender down inside all of us that wants to be thought well of even though we are not really worthy of it. So we easily succumb to this desire.

But true love, as we have been seeing, comes from the Holy Spirit. In Romans 5, Paul says, "The love of God is shed abroad in your heart by the Holy Spirit which is given unto you." True love is manifested by learning from the Word of God how you should behave in a certain situation, and then, depending on the Spirit of God to give you the strength to do it, moving out and doing that very thing. That is the way you love—by acting in obedience to what the Word tells you by the power of the Holy Spirit within you.

This is what we are exhorted to do in this passage. Verses 9 through 13 set forth love as it is manifested in the family of God, the church. Verses 14 through 21 describe how Christian love looks when it is out in the world. First, love in the church is described:

> Love must be sincere. Hate what is evil; cling to what is good. Be devoted to one another in brotherly love. Honor one another above yourselves. Never be lacking in zeal, but keep your spiritual fervor, serving the Lord. Be joyful in hope, patient in affliction, faithful in prayer. Share with God's people who are in need. Practice hospitality (vv. 9–13).

This describes love among Christians. Notice that it consists of six things which the apostle brings out very clearly. *First*, true love rejects sin, but not the person who sins. This is what Paul means when he says, "Hate what is evil; cling to what is good." He is talking about people. That is, hate what is evil in people, but don't reject the person because of the evil. The person is good. God loves him. He or she is made in the image of God. Therefore, true love learns to hate evil but not to reject the good. I grant you this is difficult to do. But hypocritical love, love that pretends to be Christian, does the opposite.

Hypocritical love is never extended to a person unless he behaves according to an acceptable standard. This is one of the things in churches that has turned people off more than anything else. People come and hear the great words of the New Testament about love and peace and joy and expect to find them exhibited, but instead they find all the world's attitudes—rejection and prejudice and even contempt. The church cuts them off and sets them aside, not wanting to have anything to do with them because they don't meet a certain standard of performance. That is what this word warns us against. It is hypocrisy to reject persons because you don't like their behavior.

But you can go to the other extreme in this, too. It is also hypocritical to condone sin because you accept the person. Christians often realize that it is wrong to cut people off and have nothing to do with them because they are not behaving properly. But some Christians accept these people and say nothing about their evil or sin, and even defend it on occasion. We are seeing something of this today in the matters of homosexuality and alcoholism. People want to defend these sins, as though they were right, simply because they want to accept the person. "Hate what is evil [loathe it]; but cling to what is good."

Second, true love remembers that relationship is the ground of concern, and not friendship. That is why Paul says, "Be devoted to one another in brotherly love." This does not refer to just anyone who is in need or in trouble; it specifies your brother or sister. The basis of concern for one another is not that we know each other well or enjoy one another; it is that we are related to one another, even though we may never have met before. If we are Christians, we already have a tie that ought to evoke concern and care for one another.

Unlimited Good

Third, Paul says that true love regards others as more deserving than yourself. "Honor one another above yourselves." I like Phillips' translation here. He says, "Be willing to let other men have the credit." That is a practical application of this. Years ago I ran across a sign that has helped me many times. I have often been on the verge of pointing out that the credit belonged to me, but I have been stopped by the remembrance of this little motto: "There is no limit to the good that a man can do if he doesn't care who gets the credit." If you really don't care who gets the credit, you can just enjoy yourself and do all kinds of good deeds. Just be glad that it is done, and don't worry about who gets the credit. Again, our flesh doesn't like that; it is very eager to be acknowledged and promoted. But the Word tells us that real love will not act that way.

Fourth, real love retains enthusiasm despite setbacks. "Never be lacking in zeal, but keep your spiritual fervor, serving the Lord." I think one of the most noticeable marks of a Christian walking in the Spirit is that he retains enthusiasm, always rejoicing, rejoicing in hope. He never lets his spiritual zeal flag or sag. After all, the one thing the Lord cannot put up with, as he tells us in the letters to the churches in Revelation, is lukewarmness. It is nauseating. He will spew you out of his mouth if you are indifferent, neither hot nor cold, just going along with the crowd. Jesus says that lukewarmness is very distressing to him.

I have always enjoyed the Old Testament story of David and Goliath. Remember how all Israel was sunk in despair because of their fear of this giant? The whole army of Israel was helpless because of the taunts of this man. But little David was fearless. Though he was only a stripling, he was not afraid. He looked at Goliath, in all his impressive height and great strength, and asked, "Who is this uncircumcized Philistine, who dares defy the armies of the living God? Who does he think he is?" Now where did David get this kind of enthusiastic response? David tells us when he says, "The battle is not ours but the Lord's."

This is what Paul is saying here. It is not your battle; it is the Lord's. It is not your resources that are required to work it out; it is his. After all, why should you be afraid or distressed or want to give up? It doesn't depend on you. You are serving the Lord! That is why it is important to note what Paul is saying here. He reminds us of this fact: the only way to keep our enthusiasm high is to be aware that we are serving the Lord.

Fifth, true love rejoices in hope. "Be joyful in hope, patient in affliction, faithful in prayer." The way to rejoice in hope is explained by the two other things mentioned here. When trials come, the thing to do is to begin with prayer. As Paul tells us in Philippians, "In everything, by prayer and supplication with thanksgiving, make your requests known unto God." Take them to him. If you are faithful in prayer, you will be able to be patient in affliction. You won't be dropping out, or copping out, or quitting, but you will be hanging in there, waiting until God works it out, not getting impatient, angry, or resentful, but quietly waiting for God to accomplish what he had in mind. That, of course, will make you rejoice in hope—because you will discover that God has a thousand and one different ways of working things out, ways that you can never imagine. That makes you begin to rejoice. You rejoice because God knows what he is doing and he is able to work it out.

Then, *sixth*, true love responds to needs. "Share with God's people who are in need. Practice hospitality." In these days when we have so much social help available—unemployment insurance, Social Security, welfare, Medicare, and so on—we tend to forget that there are still human needs and that we have a responsibility to meet them. I think we need to be reminded at times that people are still hurting and that it is a direct responsibility of Christians to care for one another's needs.

These are the ways that you manifest love in the church. Let me review them quickly for you: (1) True love rejects sin but not persons; (2) it remembers relationship is the ground of concern; (3) it regards others as more deserving than oneself; (4) it retains enthusiasm despite setbacks; (5) it rejoices in hope by being patient in affliction and faithful in prayer; and (6) it responds to needs in direct and personal ways, and especially by practicing hospitality.

Now Paul moves on to describe love exhibited to a non-Christian world. Again, he gives us six ways to do this:

> Bless those who persecute you; bless and do not curse. Rejoice with those who rejoice; mourn with those who mourn. Live in harmony with one another. Don't be proud, but be willing to associate with people of low position. Don't be conceited.

> Do not repay anyone evil for evil. Be careful to do what is right in the sight of everybody. If it is possible, as far as it depends on you, live at peace with everyone. Do not take revenge, my friends, but leave room for God's wrath, for it is written: "It is mine to avenge, I will repay," says the Lord. On the contrary: "If your enemy is hungry, feed him; if he is

thirsty, give him something to drink. In doing this, you will heap burning coals on his head." Do not be overcome by evil, but overcome evil with good (vv. 14–21).

First, love speaks well of its persecutors. That is a tough one, isn't it? "Bless those who persecute you; bless and do not curse." That is getting right down to where the rubber meets the road! It means you do not go around badmouthing people who are not nice to you. You don't run them down or speak harshly about them to others, but you speak well of them. You find something that you can approve, and you say so to others.

I confess that that is not my natural reaction. When someone persecutes me, I persecute back! At least I want to. But this is what the Word tells us we don't need to do and should not do. I think this applies even to such practical areas as traffic problems. Have you ever been persecuted in traffic? It happens all the time. Someone cuts you off, and you want to roll down the window and shout, "Melonhead!" But according to this passage, you are not supposed to react this way. Now, this doesn't tell you what to call them, but it does tell you to bless them.

Rejoicing Is Harder

Second, true love adjusts to other people's moods. "Rejoice with those who rejoice; mourn with those who mourn." When someone in your office is feeling low and gloomy, don't come in and sit down and whistle away. When they obviously don't respond, don't ask, "What's the matter with you? How come you're so down all the time? Why don't you be cheerful like me?" There is nothing worse than a cheerful person when something has gone wrong for you. No, Paul says, adjust yourself. Mourn with those who mourn, and rejoice with those who rejoice. I think he puts rejoicing first because that is so hard to do sometimes—especially if it awakens our envy or self-pity. If someone else has achieved something that we think we ought to have, it is hard to go up to that person and say, "I'm so glad for you." But that is what love does, and it is possible to do it—for those who walk in the Spirit.

Third, true love does not show partiality. Paul says very precisely, "Live in harmony with one another. Don't be proud, but be willing to associate with people of low position. Don't be conceited." When Jesus came to Jerusalem he stayed with Mary and Martha and Lazarus out in the little suburban town of Bethany instead of at the Intercontinental Hotel in Jerusalem. This is the attitude the apostle enjoins Christians to have. And he suggests that the real reason for respecting persons and for namedropping and that kind of thing is really personal conceit. "Don't be conceited," he says. "Don't think highly of yourself." That is what makes you always want to be associated with the upper echelons of society. But if you have an honest view of yourself, you know that you are no better than anyone else and therefore you will be willing just to enjoy the ordinary people. And you will find a rich manifestation of love and humanity among them.

Fourth, love is not sneaky or underhanded (v. 17). Paul tells us not to give back evil for evil, but to plan to do right, out in the open, before all. "Do not repay anyone evil for evil. Be careful to do what is right in the sight of everybody." Here Paul is telling us not to take silent revenge for imagined or real insults and not to resort to subterfuges to get even.

Fifth, true love seeks to live at peace with everyone. "If it is possible, as far as it depends on you, live at peace with everyone." There are people who just will not allow you to be at peace with them, but don't let it start with you. Remember the old song, "It Takes Two to Tango"? I think that last word ought to be "tangle." It takes two to tangle. If you refuse to tangle, at least the conflict does not depend on you and is not traceable to your actions and your attitudes. That is what love really does.

Escalated Conflict

Then, *sixth,* love does not try to get even. Listen to these words again. "Do not take revenge, my friends, but leave room for God's wrath, for it is written, 'It is mine to avenge,

I will repay,' says the Lord." Revenge is one of the most
natural of human responses to hurt or injury or bad attitudes. We always feel that if we treat others according to
the way they have treated us we are only treating them as
they deserve. We can justify this so easily. "I'm only teaching them a lesson. I'm only showing them how I feel. I'm
only giving back what they've given me." But any time you
argue that way you have forgotten the many times you have
injured others without getting caught yourself. But God
hasn't forgotten. This always puts us in the place of those
Pharisees who, when the woman was taken in adultery, were
ready to stone her to death. Jesus said to them, "He that is
without sin among you, let him cast the first stone." That
stopped them all dead in their tracks, because there wasn't
one of them who was not equally guilty. They needed to be
judged, too. We must never carry out revenge, because we
are not in the position of a judge. Since we too are guilty,
we need to be judged. Therefore, Paul's admonition is,
"Don't try to avenge yourself." You will only make a mess
of it. The inevitable result of trying to get even with people
is that you escalate the conflict. It is inescapable.

As a boy in Montana I used to watch the cows in the corral. They would be standing there peacefully and then one
cow would kick another cow. Of course, that cow had to
kick back. Then the first cow kicked harder and missed the
second cow and hit a third. That cow kicked back. I
watched that happen many times. One single cow, starting
to kick another, soon had the whole corral kicking and
milling and mooing at one another, mad as could be. This
happens in congregations, too.

Paul gives two reasons why you should not avenge yourself. One is because God is already doing it. "Leave room
for God's wrath." God knows you have been insulted or hurt
or injured. He knows it and he is already doing something
about it. Second, God alone claims the right to vengeance
because he alone can work it without injury to all concerned.
Since he will do it in a way that will be redemptive, he
won't injure the other person, but will bring him out of it.

Too often we fail to give God a chance; we take the matter into our own hands. Paul says such an action is wrong because we don't want that person to be redeemed; we want him to be hurt. We are like Jonah when Nineveh repented. When God spared the city, Jonah became angry with God. "Why didn't you wipe them out like you said you would?" Paul reminds us that God is already avenging, so we should leave him room. God claims the right to vengeance because he alone can work it without injury to all concerned.

You ask, "What do you expect me to do? Somebody hits me—do you expect me just to sit there and do nothing?" Oh no, there is something you can do. Look what it is: "On the contrary: 'If your enemy is hungry, feed him; if he is thirsty, give him something to drink. In doing this, you will heap burning coals on his head.' Do not be overcome by evil, but overcome evil with good" (vv. 20,21).

To Make Him Ashamed

Two things will happen if you refuse to avenge yourself and let God do it. First, you will be enabled to act positively instead of negatively. That will result in what Paul, quoting Proverbs 25:21,22, calls "heaping burning coals on his head." This does not mean that you are going to get even by another process—burning his head. This refers to the ancient way of lighting fires. They did not have matches in those days, so if you wanted to light a fire in your home you couldn't go and simply borrow a match. But you could go and borrow some coals from your neighbor. Of course, you took along an earthen jar that would not burn. Then you would ask your neighbor if you could borrow some coals to light your own fire. Now, if he was a good neighbor, he would fill the jar and you would carry the padded jar home on top of your head. This became a picture of an ample, generous response to a neighbor's need. After awhile it became a metaphor for responding so generously to your neighbor that it made him ashamed of himself for his attitude toward you. That is what Paul is suggesting here.

The second result of leaving vengeance to God is that you

win the battle. If there is a conflict going on you will win
it if you respond by doing good instead of evil. One day I
read a story about a boy who was in the army. He was a
Christian and had formed the habit of praying beside his
bed before he went to sleep. He kept up this practice in
the army, but he became an object of mockery and ridicule
to the entire barracks. One night he knelt to pray after a
long, weary march. As he was praying, one of his tormentors
took off his muddy boots and threw them at the boy, one at
a time, hitting him on each side of his head. Saying nothing
about it, the Christian just took the boots and put them beside his bed and continued to pray. But the next morning,
when the other man woke up, he found his boots sitting beside his bed, all shined and polished. It so broke his heart
that he came to the boy and asked him for forgiveness. That
led, after a time, to the man becoming a Christian. This is
what Paul means when he says you overcome evil with good.

Three times in this passage the apostle has stressed the
fact that you are not to return evil for evil. In verses 14, 17,
and 21 he states it. So, throughout this passage it is under-
scored that the major way we express love in the world is
by not reacting in vengeance when we are mistreated by the
world. Can you imagine what would happen if Christians
would begin to act this way? How many times do we turn
people away from Christianity by assuming the same attitude as the world around us? Surely this is a practical way
Paul has of reminding us that we are not to be conformed to
this age. We are not to think like they do. It is recorded of
the Lord Jesus that when he was reviled, "he reviled not
again, but committed himself to him who judges all things
righteously." That was given for our admonition, that we
might behave as Jesus did in the midst of the world. What a
testimony of grace that would be!

10

God's Strange Servants

Our study of the Book of Romans has brought us to the famous passage in chapter 13 that deals with the Christian and his relationship to the government. It is not difficult to think of President Jimmy Carter as a servant of God. His personal profession of a new birth has been well publicized. But have you ever thought of Leonid Brezhnev as a servant of God? Or Idi Amin? Or even Adolph Hitler? And yet, amazingly, this passage declares that men like these are, in some sense, servants of God.

The first thing the apostle tells us about government is its source. Where does it originate? The answer is given in the very first verse:

> Everyone must submit himself to the governing authorities, for there is no authority except that which God has established. The authorities that exist have been established by God.

When Paul refers to "governing authorities," he uses a phrase that can best be translated "the powers that be." He is not just talking about heads of state; he is talking about all levels of authority, all the way down to the local dogcatcher. These are the powers that be, those that exist. We must

realize that these governmental offices are in some way
brought into being by God himself.

No Best Form

I often hear people ask, "Which form of government is the
best? Which is the one God wants us to have?" We Americans would love to think that democracy is the most God-
honored form of government. But I don't think you can
establish that from the Scriptures. In fact, the Scriptures
support various forms of government. You may ask, "Which
government is the best kind? Is it a monarchy? An oligarchy
(i.e., rule by a few)? Is it a republic? A democracy? The
answer of Scripture is not necessarily any of these. It is
whatever God has brought into being. This is best for the
particular place and time in history. God has brought it into
being, considering the makeup of the people, the degree of
truth and light which is disseminated among them, and the
moral conditions that prevail. For that condition, for that
time and place, God has brought into being a particular
government.

Now, that government can change. God does not ordain
any one form of government to be continued forever. If the
people grow toward understanding of truth, and morality
prevails in a community, the form of government may well
take on a democratic posture. Where truth disappears, government seems to become more autocratic. But in any case,
the point the apostle makes is that whatever form of government you find, God is behind it. Therefore, we need to see
that no government is in itself opposed to God. That includes communism as much as any other form of government.

This truth is not confined to the New Testament. In the
book of Daniel, just before Daniel was to go before Nebuchadnezzar—one of the most autocratic of kings—he prayed
to God and said, "Blessed be the name of God for ever and
ever. . . . He changes times and seasons; he removes kings
and sets up kings" (Dan. 2:20,21 RSV). There it is made clear
that God definitely has a hand in whatever is going on at

any particular time on the earth. Sometimes we are tempted or even taught to think of God as being remote from our political affairs, but Scripture never takes that position. God is not on some distant Mount Olympus; he is right among us, involved in the pattern of governments. He raises up kings and puts down others, raises up rulers and changes forms of government.

I think we Americans are slowly learning that not every body of people in the world can handle democracy. There was a time when we naively thought democracy was the best and only enlightened form of government, and all we had to do was go around the world and set up democracies and people would begin to function properly. Democracy would solve all their problems. Now, after many painful experiences, we know better than that. We know there are times and places where democracy just will not work; people are not ready for it. They can't handle that kind of liberty, that kind of responsibility, so God does not give it to them. The government they have is better suited for their purpose than ours would be.

When Paul wrote this letter, these Christians were living in the capital city of the empire, Rome itself. By this time Rome had already passed through several forms of government. It had been a monarchy, a republic, a principate, and now it was an empire. Nero had just begun his reign as the fifth emperor of Rome. What Paul is saying to these Christians is that whatever form of government may be in control, they are to remember that God is behind it.

Bad Men Too

Not only is God behind the forms of government we have, but he is also responsible for the incumbents, the ones occupying the offices at any particular time. That may be a startling thought for some of us, but it is what this verse says. Here is how the New English Bible translates the last half of verse 1: "There is no authority but by act of God, and the existing authorities are instituted by him." Not only are the forms of government brought into being by God, but the very people who occupy the offices are put there by God.

So if you thank God for Jimmy Carter and say that God gave us a godly, born-again President, remember that he also gave us Richard Nixon, Spiro Agnew, and all the others with whom we have had some trouble. They came from God, too. God is neither a Republican nor a Democrat. He is not a socialist, or a Marxist, or even an American! The biblical picture is that God not only sends us good men sometimes, by his grace, to lead us and heal us, but he also sends us bad men at times, to punish us. And we deserve them. Therefore, when Hitlers, Stalins, and other ruthless individuals come to the throne of power, God has put them there because they are what people needed at that particular time in history.

This is the biblical position with regard to government, and it is rather startling. And yet, it is the clear statement of this passage, as well as other passages of Scripture. Peter says we are to "honor the king" (1 Peter 2:17). When Peter wrote this, Nero was seated on the throne. Christians are to be subject to the governing authorities, Peter tells us. Back in the Book of Daniel we are taught the same thing. Nebuchadnezzar had been brought low before God by God's dealings with him. In a great decree, which he had issued throughout his kingdom, he testified to that effect. He said God had taught him painful lessons until he learned "that the Most High rules the kingdom of men, and gives it to whom he will" (Dan. 4:25 RSV). So the first thing we need to recognize is that regardless of the form of government we may be up against, the hand of God is in it. And not only is this true of the form of government, but also of the very ones who occupy the positions of power. God has put them there.

The second thing we need to know about our relationship to government is found in verse 2:

> Consequently, he who rebels against the authority is rebelling against what God has instituted, and those who do so will bring judgment on themselves.

Clearly, if God is behind governments, then those who oppose the government and would overthrow it are really opposing God. I realize this has to be handled very carefully, because there are those who would use a statement like this to justify everything the government does—no matter what it is. But we must recognize, first of all, that governments do have a God-given right to punish those who would overthrow them—to punish treason, to control riots, and to seek to preserve themselves in power by legitimate means. Governments do have that right.

Punishment within Limits

But, though Paul does not go into this aspect of it in this particular passage, we must also remember the Scriptures show us that such a right is always held under God. I thank God for the enlightened soul who, a few decades ago, began the movement to add the words "under God" to our pledge of allegiance. That reflects biblical truth. This nation exists as a nation under God. That means we are to recognize that we have limited power. We are agents of God, but we are not God.

There are some things that nations have no right to do. The Bible is clear on what those kinds of things are. This is what Jesus clearly referred to in that famous incident when he was asked about paying taxes. He held up a coin and asked, "Whose image is on the coin?" His audience said, "Caesar's." He said, "All right, then give to Caesar the things that belong to Caesar; but give God the things that belong to God." By this he clearly indicated that there are limits to the power of government. Caesar has his image on certain things; therefore they belong to him—and rightfully so. What Caesar put his image on belongs to Caesar. But God has put his image on men; they belong to him. So men may give certain *things* to Caesar, but the *men* themselves belong to God and should rightfully give themselves to him.

Governments have authority over what we do with our property and how we behave with one another, but our

Lord clearly indicates they have no right to touch that upon which God has put his image. This is the spirit of man. In other words, Caesar has no right to command the worship of man or forbid his obedience to the Word of God. Rulers are under God; therefore they have no right to command men to do what God says ought not to be done or to command men not to do what God says should be done. These are the limits of governmental powers. Governments are not to enslave men, because men belong to God. Governments are not to oppress men, because men bear the image of God. What bears God's image must be given to God, and not to Caesar—just as what bears Caesar's image must be given to Caesar, and not necessarily to God. Though this passage doesn't deal at length with this, it indicates clearly that believers have a right to resist oppression and religious persecution by nonviolent means as they have opportunity. But they are not to resist the legitimate functions of government. We are to accept government as a gift of God.

The legitimate functions of government are further described for us in verse 3:

> For rulers hold no terror for those who do right, but for those who do wrong. Do you want to be free from fear of the one in authority? Then do what is right and he will commend you.

Do you hear what Paul is saying? If you are driving down the freeway and want to be free from having to look constantly in your rearview mirror, then keep the speed down! The officer will pull you aside and say, "Sir, you were driving so beautifully that I just want to commend you." Well, no, he won't do that. He may wish he had time to, but he will just pass by and wave at you. Verse 4 says:

> For he is God's servant to do you good. But if you do wrong, be afraid, for he does not bear the sword for nothing. He is God's servant, an agent of justice to bring punishment on the wrongdoer.

To Preserve Security

In this very helpful passage, we learn that government has two basic functions. First, governments are to protect us from evil; that is, they are to preserve the security of people. They are to protect us from attack from without and crime from within. For that purpose, governments properly have armies and police systems and courts of justice to preserve us from evil in our midst.

Then in verse 6 we have another function of government:

> This is why you pay taxes, for the authorities are God's servants, who give their full time to governing.

Notice that in these three verses Paul calls government agents "the servants of God" three times. The first two times, in verses 3 and 4, he uses the word in Greek from which we get our word "deacon." They are the deacons of God. The next time you are called up in traffic court you must view the judge as a deacon of God. He is a servant.

The point these verses make is that these authorities exist as an arm of God's work among men. This not only involves punishment of crime and wrongdoing, but also commendation. Governments are to honor those who live as good citizens. Occasionally you hear of rewards offered for those who have a record of keeping the law.

Even courts often recognize the right motives of people. Not long ago I read about a man who was hauled into court because he had stolen a loaf of bread. When the judge investigated he found out that the man had no job, his family was hungry, he had tried to get work but couldn't, tried to get funds for relief but couldn't, and so in order to feed his family he had stolen a loaf of bread. When the judge learned of the circumstances, he said, "I'm sorry, but the law can make no exceptions. You stole, and therefore I have to punish you. I have to assess a fine of ten dollars. But I want to pay the money myself." He reached into his pocket, pulled out a ten dollar bill, and handed it to the man. As soon as

the man took the money, the judge said, "Now, I also want
to remit the fine." That is, the man could keep the money.
"Furthermore, I am going to instruct the bailiff to pass a
hat to everyone in this courtroom, and I am fining everybody
fifty cents for living in a city where a man has to steal in
order to have bread to eat." When the money was collected,
he gave it to the defendant.

That represents the good side of justice, a court that will,
on occasion, recognize the right motives of people, even
though there may be wrongdoing involved. That is a legitimate function of government. The government also has the
right "to provide for the common defense, and insure do-
mestic tranquility," as the Constitution phrases it.

To Serve As Priests

A second basic function of government is indicated in
verse 6, in the word used for "servants." It is not the word
"deacon" here; it is "priest." The idea here is that the government is not only to provide for our defense and security, but
also to provide certain common services that we all need—
to function as priests among us, helping us in our needs. Out
of this grows the governmental functions of providing mail
service, utilities (water, sewage), schools, relief agencies,
and so on. These are all proper functions of government
agencies.

By God's grace, governments have two powers which enable them to provide these services. First, they have the
authority to use force. That is what is meant by "he bears
not the sword for nothing." The sword is the symbol of the
right to use force, even to the point of taking life.

I don't think there is any area today in which people are
more confused and muddled in their thinking than in this
area of the government's right to use force. Take the question of capital punishment, for example. What people need
to understand is that when the state, acting in line with the
judicial system, functioning as it was intended to function,
finally passes sentence on an individual to yield his life for a

certain crime, that is really not the same thing as a man taking another man's life. God is taking that life by means of the state. We need to remember that God has the right to take human life. All through the Old Testament you find him doing that very thing. He also has the right to set up human channels for doing this. This means that governments have the basic right to maintain armies for their defense, and that people—even Christians—are to serve in them.

Of course there is no question but that these powers can be and have been abused. Citizens have every right to protest these abuses and to seek to correct them. But it is folly to try to eliminate the rightful uses of authority simply because some of them are being abused. What we should do is to correct the abuses and not eliminate the things Scripture ordains.

The second power this passage says governments rightfully have from God is the power to collect taxes. You may not like the amount of taxes that your government collects, but you can't object to the principle of taxation. Taxes are right, and governments have taxed their citizens from time immemorial, and will continue to do so. The apostle makes clear that the government has the right to collect taxes, and Christians should pay them.

Because of Conscience

The final position of the Christian with respect to these things is summed up in verses 5 and 7. In verse 5 we see the attitude we are to have:

> Therefore, it is necessary to submit to the authorities, not only because of possible punishment but also because of conscience.

This has to do with our attitude about taxes, arrests, judicial systems, and so on. We are to obey the law not just because we are afraid of getting caught. We are to keep to the speed limit not just because there is a police car in sight. We are to pay our income taxes, not only because we know the government has tremendous computers that can review any number of records and might catch us. That is a factor, and many more people are honest today about their taxes because of it, but that ought not to be the Christian's reason for being honest in paying his taxes. The Christian's reason is that it is the right thing to do before God. Your conscience ought to be clear. You ought to pay the taxes because this is what God says to do, and not what man says.

Then verse 7 tells us what actual actions ought to follow:

> Give everyone what you owe him; if you owe taxes, pay taxes; if revenue, then revenue [Revenue refers to those hidden taxes such as sales taxes, customs duties, etc.]; if respect, then respect; if honor, then honor.

Here the apostle is dealing with our actual response to these demands of government. We haven't the right to withhold taxes if the government doesn't use them quite the way we think they should. Governments are made up of fallible men and women just like us, and we can't demand that the government always handle everything perfectly. Therefore what Paul wrote to these Romans, who had the same problems we have about taxes, was, "If you owe taxes, pay them."

The point the apostle is making here is: do not resent these powers of government. This is all set within the context of Paul's word in chapter 12, "Be not conformed to this present age." Don't act as everyone else acts about taxes. The world grumbles and gripes and groans at paying taxes. You have a right, of course, as does everyone, to protest injustice and to correct abuse, but don't forever be grumbling about the taxes that you have to pay.

I have had to learn some lessons on this myself. The first time I had to pay an income tax was a few years ago. My income had been so low for a long time that I didn't have to pay any taxes. But gradually it caught up and I finally had to pay. I remember how I resented it. In fact, when I sent my tax form in I addressed it to "The Infernal Revenue Service." They never answered, although they did accept the money. The next year, I had improved my attitude a bit. I addressed it to "The Eternal Revenue Service." But I have repented from all those sins, and I now hope to pay my taxes cheerfully.

I do not attempt to defend the gross injustices that prevail in our American system. But the very fact that we can meet openly together to worship God, the very fact that we have relative freedom from attack when we walk about, is due to the existence of a government that God has brought into being. I want to make every effort I can, as a good citizen, to improve it and to see that it does things better. But I thank God for the privilege of paying taxes.

Someone has well said, "Every nation gets the government it deserves." And so as we pay our taxes, let us do so cheerfully. Remember the apostle says not only that we are to pay our taxes, but if we owe respect, we are to give that; if honor, give that. Never forget that the worst governments are, nevertheless, better than anarchy, and serve certain functions which God himself has ordained. Therefore let us respond as Christians, with cheerfulness and gladness for what we can do under God, with such an attitude that people will see that there is something different about us. Thus we commend ourselves to God and the people around.

11

The Night Is Nearly Over

When Paul wrote this letter, surely love was the thing most lacking in the Roman empire. These Christians needed desperately to learn how to display love amidst the pressure and oppression of that day. This was what was needed in the city of Corinth, with its immoral sexual practices and its abandonment to pleasure—the city from which Paul wrote the letter to the Romans. In the midst of seeking after merriment and pleasure the Corinthians needed to learn the gift of love. The greatest need of men anywhere today is to learn the secret of how to love. Love makes a difference.

Listen to what Paul says to these Romans in chapter 13:

> Let no debt remain outstanding, except the continuing debt to love one another, for he who loves his fellow man has fulfilled the law. The commandments, "Do not commit adultery," "Do not murder," "Do not steal," "Do not covet," and whatever other commandment there may be, are summed up in this one rule: "Love your neighbor as yourself." Love does no harm to its neighbor. Therefore love is the fulfillment of the law (vv. 8–10).

Have you ever struggled to obey the Ten Commandments? Have you found it difficult to face up to obeying these demands that you shall not murder or lie or steal or commit adultery? Well, Paul says it is really easy. All you have to do is love. Act in love toward people and you won't hurt them. You can't. Love is the solution to all the problems we struggle with. Have you ever thought of what would happen in this world if people could be taught how to love—and then did it?

The first result that occurs to me is that all the impending divorces would soon be happily resolved. Couples ready to split up because love has left their marriage could go back together and learn how to work it out. Think what would happen if all the divorce problems pending in this country would suddenly be resolved and homes and families would be secure!

If we could teach people how to love we would not fight wars. We wouldn't have to worry about disarmament. We could send the atom bombs and nuclear explosives and missiles off into space somewhere and let them join the rest of the space garbage. What a remarkable thing that would be! Think of how much energy and money is being expended in keeping up this endless array of armaments simply because we can't trust people to love each other.

If we could love each other, there wouldn't be any more crime. The streets would be safe for pedestrians once more, and in all the great cities of our land we would feel safe and secure—if people would learn to love. Of course, if there weren't any crime, we wouldn't need any prisons. All the money we spend on prisons and reformatories could be spent on something more useful. And you wouldn't need any courts of law or police—except to regulate traffic a little now and then. We need all these things because we are deprived of this ability to love.

And think what would happen to our tax burden if we could get rid of all wars and crimes and police and courts! Taxes would be reduced to practically nothing! All the money poured into taxes today could be used to spread beauty and harmony of life to everyone on earth. Clearly, our biggest problem is our lack of love, our inability to love one another.

This passage is telling us that the ability to love—that and nothing less than that—is the radical force Jesus Christ has turned loose in this world by his resurrection. It has the power to radically change the world. Paul implies that this change has to start with us. If we are Christians, if we know Jesus Christ, we have the power to love. There is no doubt about that. If you know him, then you have the power to love. You don't have to ask for it; you've got it. If you have Christ, you have the ability to act in love, even though you are tempted not to.

The Debt You Owe

Therefore, Paul says, when you rub shoulders with people, remember that your first obligation is to love them. Act in love. Show courtesy, kindness, patience, understanding, longsuffering—whatever it takes, whatever the scene demands, you can show that. It is a debt you owe that person. "Owe no man anything but to love one another." Paul says plainly that we are to think of this as our obligation to everyone. I wonder what kinds of radical things would start happening among us if we were to start living on this basis, if we would say to ourselves every day, every time we meet someone, "I need to show love to this person. No matter what else happens, I have an obligation to pay him that debt."

I have noticed that whenever I meet people to whom I owe money the first thing that comes to my mind is the debt I owe them, and I wonder if that is what they are thinking about, too! Paul says we are to think about love in this way. We are to remember that we have an obligation to love.

The second thing Paul says is that this obligation is to everyone. This is intended for your neighbor. Who is your neighbor? You think immediately of the people who live on each side of you. They are your neighbors, because they live next door to you. They are in contact with you. But you can see that many others are in contact with you as well. The people sitting next to you in church are your neighbors, for the moment at least, and so are the people you meet in business, and in your shopping. Wherever you are, the people you meet are your neighbors for that moment. The word to us is that since we have the ability to love, we are to love our neighbor as ourselves. The butcher, the baker, the Cadillac maker—it doesn't make any difference, they are your neighbors.

Beyond the Law

The third thing Paul says is that when you love like this you fulfill the law and even go beyond the law. The law says to you, "Don't injure your neighbor." You can do what you like with your own property, but it stops at your neighbor's line. You can't do what you like with his. If you do, you are answerable to the law. But you see, love goes a step beyond that. It doesn't stop with the negative, "Don't injure your neighbor"; it says, "Do good to your neighbor." Love him, reach out to him, minister to him, help him. It is simply impossible to love your neighbor and harm him at the same time.

Thus, as Paul says, love will not sleep with your neighbor's wife or husband. Love will not murder your neighbor, or poison his dog, or throw garbage over the fence into his back yard, or do anything harmful to him. Love will not steal from your neighbor, or even keep his lawn mower for more than a month. Love will not covet what is your neighbor's, it won't drool over his pool, or stew about his new Porsche. Love does not want what your neighbor has, but rejoices with him over what he has. Love, therefore, fulfills the law. You don't have to worry about keeping the Ten Commandments; all you have to worry about is acting in love, paying the debt you owe every man, every woman, every child, every person you meet. If you pay them the debt of love you will not injure them.

Furthermore, Paul says:

And do this, understanding the present time. The hour has come for you to wake up from your slumber, because our

salvation is nearer now than when we first believed. The night
is nearly over; the day is almost here. So let us put aside the
deeds of darkness and put on the armor of light. Let us behave
decently, as in the daytime, not in orgies and drunkenness, not
in sexual immorality and debauchery, not in dissension and
jealousy. Rather, clothe yourselves with the Lord Jesus Christ,
and do not think about how to gratify the desires of your
sinful nature (vv. 11–14).

The thing that strikes me about this paragraph is the opening words. Love your neighbor, Paul says, pay the debt you
owe him, "understanding the present time." There is something about the age in which we live, if you understand it,
which will compel you, motivate you, drive you to love your
neighbor. If you understand the times, you will be helped
to do this.

Paul points out three things about the times. First, he says
it is time to get going: "The hour has come for you to wake
up from your slumber, because our salvation is nearer now
than when we first believed. The night is nearly over; the
day is almost here."

It is time to wake up, time to get going, time to look
around and recognize all the opportunities to love. I am
amazed to see how many times in my own life I pass over
an opportunity to love. I am always looking for opportunities
with other people out there, further away. Yet I am surrounded in my own family with opportunities to show love,
even when it is difficult. Christians are called to love the
unlovely, those who, for the moment, are not themselves
acting in love. How easy it is for people to want to help
someone farther away and ignore the needs right around
them. A couple brought some clothes down to our church
one day to take to the Rescue Mission. The lady was very
concerned about the poor people's need for proper clothing,
but I noticed that her husband had to hold his pants up
with a nail!

Now, we don't have much time to do this reaching out.
The time is short. As Paul puts it, "Our salvation is nearer
than when we first believed." That is, the deliverance for

which we are looking, when Christ returns again, is nearer than when we first believed. No one can argue with that. The Christian message has been going out for 1900 years— and how much nearer we are to the time when Christ is coming back! There is no doubt about it. "The night is nearly over," Paul says, "the day is almost here." On one occasion Jesus said, "I must work the works of my Father while it is day. The night is coming, when no man can work." Jesus was aware of the urgency of the time, and the fact that he had to labor because the day was almost gone. On another occasion he said, "As long as I am in the world, I am the light of the world." That is what created the day. When Jesus was present on earth, then it was daytime. But when he left us physically, when he was buried in the grave, the night came. The night has been running on now for more than 1900 years. As the apostle Paul tells us in his letter to the Colossians, "We Christians are to be like lights shining in the darkness of the night." The night is all around us, but the day is about to come. The night is nearly over; the day is at hand.

The Edge of Eternity

You say, "Wait a minute. Paul wrote this letter 1900 years ago, and he said it was nearly over then. How could it have been nearly over then, when 1900 years have gone by?" When you look at it from that point of view, it is difficult to understand. But there is a sense here in which these words are always true of every one of us. I am sure this is the way the apostle meant them for himself. Regardless of whether or not this is the generation in which Jesus Christ returns to fulfill his promise, the truth is that the night is nearly over for every one of us, for when our brief life ends the day dawns.

For those of us who have a few gray hairs, the night is nearly over; the day is at hand. If we are ever going to love, it has to be now. We can't wait much longer. But how about young people, fresh and strong and filled with excitement and energy? I often think of the words of George Bernard Shaw: "Youth is such a wonderful thing, it's a shame to waste it on the young." But how much time do young people have? Who knows? We all live on the edge of eternity. The night may be nearly over for any one of us, no matter whether we are old or young. So the argument of the apostle is powerful. He is saying, "If you are going to love, now is the time to do it. You can't wait for tomorrow. You can't plan on doing this after you graduate from school. Start now. Now you must begin to love one another. The night is nearly over; the day is at hand."

The second thing we need to understand is that the present is the time to give up.

> So let us put aside the deeds of darkness and put on the armor of light. Let us behave decently, as in the daytime, not in orgies and drunkenness, not in sexual immorality and debauchery, not in dissension and jealousy (vv. 13,14).

If you are going to live in love, then certain things must go. Some things are incompatible with love. You can't do them and love at the same time. Paul suggests three categories:

The *first* is, "Don't live for empty and harmful pleasures. Give up orgies and drunkenness." That covers a whole spectrum of things and means, "Don't devote your life to seeking good times, things that you plan over and over again for your own self-indulgence, an endless round of parties or plays or concerts, opera, or even watching television." You can't love and do that. Such a course is wasting your life. You have only so many precious moments to show this mighty power, this release, this radical power of love. If you spend your moments in endless self-indulgence you will never be able to live in love.

Too Easily Pleased

Second, "Don't live for sex." Sex is a powerful force that is highly exploited today. We are constantly surrounded with silken and sensuous temptations—a new love affair, a new

romance, a new sexual liaison will satisfy us, please us, fulfill us. The world urges us to try it; there is no harm in it,
they tell us. But Paul says there is. He says if you live for
these things, you can't fulfill what God wants you to fulfill.
So doing will cause you to miss the excitement and the radical glory of loving people. You can't love people and live for
sex. Paul covers the whole range of immorality here—forni-
cation, adultery, homosexuality, pornography. You can't indulge in these things and love; you will hurt people and you
will hurt yourself. You will destroy others and destroy yourself. This is so essential that to experience the glory of what
God wants you have to lay aside these cheapened, tawdry
things. I like what C. S. Lewis says:

> We are half-hearted creatures, fooling around with drink and
> sex and ambition, when infinite joy is offered us. Like an
> ignorant child who wants to go on making mud pies in a slum
> because he cannot imagine what is meant by the offer of a
> holiday at the sea, we are far too easily pleased.

The *third* category is this: "Don't live for strife, causing
dissension and jealousy." It is amazing to me how many
people, including Christians, get their kicks out of being the
cause of dissension. They can't seem to enjoy themselves
unless they get people fighting and upset and angry—either
with them or with one another. I remember a word of Jesus
which has always helped me very much when I am tempted
along these lines. He said, "He that is with me gathers; but
he that is against me scatters." What is your effect upon people? Do you harmonize them? Do you gather them together?
Are they noticeably happier because you have come in? Or
do strife, division, and separation immediately break out
when you are there? What is your life doing? This is the
way you can tell whether you are with Jesus or against him.
If you are with him, you gather people; if you are against
him, you scatter them.

So Paul says it is time not only to get going, and time to
give up, but it is time to put on, above all else:

Rather, clothe yourselves with the Lord Jesus Christ, and do not think about how to gratify the desires of your sinful nature (v. 14).

When I get up in the morning I put on my clothes, intending them to be part of me all day, to go where I go and do what I do. They cover me and make me presentable to others. That is the purpose of clothes. In the same way, the apostle is saying to us, "Put on Jesus Christ when you get up in the morning. Make him a part of your life that day. Intend that he go with you everywhere you go, and that he act through you in everything you do. Call upon his resources. Live your life *IN CHRIST*." That is the way to love.

Notice that Paul uses the full name, "the Lord Jesus Christ." I think he does this deliberately. "Lord" stands for his power to rule, his authority, his power to change and alter events, to control history, "to open, and no man shuts; to shut, and no man opens." When you put on Jesus Christ, you are putting on power to change events and affect people that you would not have without him.

Remember that when you put on Jesus you are putting on the capacity to love. Read the gospels and you will find that the striking thing about Jesus of Nazareth was his ability to love. He would put his hand on a loathsome leper to heal him, even though the law forbade that. Jesus would reach out to the lost woman and the drunkard and speak a healing word in their lives. He treated the lowly the same as he did the higher-ups. Our Lord loved people. Everywhere people were struck with his compassion. When you put on Jesus, that is what you are putting on—the capacity to love.

When you put on Christ, you are putting on the power to deliver. Christ means "Messiah," or, "anointed." It refers to his work: Christ came to deliver us, to set us free. When you put on Christ, you have an amazing power to free yourself and others from despair in the midst of difficult circumstances. So put on the Lord Jesus Christ. Remind yourself of his presence all through the day. Reckon on his power to supply love when you begin to obey the command to love. And, as Paul says, "Do not think about how to gratify the desires of your sinful nature." Stop planning for evil and self-indulgence. That always ends in strife and rivalry, jealousy and debauchery. Rather, learn to love by putting on the Lord Jesus Christ.

"Take and Read"

These words have been made famous by their connection with the conversion of Saint Augustine. Augustine was a young man in the fourth century who was what we would call a swinger. He lived a wild, carousing life, running around with evil companions, doing everything they were doing. The young man denied himself nothing, went into anything and everything. And, as people still do today, he came to hate himself for it. One day he was with his friend in a garden, and he walked up and down, bemoaning his inability to change. "O, tomorrow, tomorrow, tomorrow! How can I free myself from these terrible urges within me that drive me to the things that hurt me!" And in his despair, as he walked in the garden, he suddenly heard what he thought was the voice of a child—perhaps some children were playing in the garden next door—and the voice said, "Take and read, take and read." He could not remember any children's games with words like that, but the words stuck. Turning back to a table in the garden, he found a copy of Paul's letter to the Romans lying there. Flipping it open, he reads these words:

> Let us behave decently, as in the daytime, not in orgies and drunkenness, not in sexual immorality and debauchery, not in dissension and jealousy. Rather, clothe yourselves with the Lord Jesus Christ . . . (vv. 13,14).

Augustine said that at that moment he opened his life to Christ. He had known about him, but had never surrendered to him. But at that moment he did, and he felt a healing touch from Christ cleansing his life. He was never the same man again.

A short time ago Eldridge Cleaver told me about his days

as a Black Panther. He said that while he was a Black Panther he was filled with a terrible feeling of hatred and
violence against any law enforcement agent. He couldn't
help himself. Every time he was with them he would feel a
murderous rage within him. Because of it, he became a
leader of the Black Panthers, the violent black militants of
the '60s. But in 1976, in the south of France, on a balcony
overlooking the Mediterranean Sea, he had a vision, an
inner view, of the face of Jesus Christ. It drove him to read
the Scriptures, and he read Psalm 23 over and over again.
He said that ever since that time on the balcony he has
never had that feeling of hatred again. He has looked for it,
expected it, but instead there has been a feeling of love for
everyone he meets.

That is what Jesus Christ is capable of doing. He gives us
all the power to love. If we but choose to exercise this power
in the moment of need we can release in the world this radical force that has the power to change everything around us.
It will change our homes, our lives, our communities, our
nations, the world—because a risen Lord is available to us,
to live through us.

J. B. Phillips' translation of this last verse puts it beautifully: "Let us be Christ's men from head to foot, and give
no chance to the flesh to have its fling." That is the way to
live.

12

On Trying to Change Others

In the fourteenth chapter of Romans Paul discusses the favorite indoor sport of Christians: trying to change each other. All through the history of the church, this problem has arisen. It comes from the attitude that God is clearly pleased with the way *we* live—but there are those *others* around! They drink beer and play cards; they go to movies; they smoke cigars; they work on Sundays; they wear lipstick; they dance; they play musical instruments; they use zippers instead of buttons—there is no end to the list.

We are dealing, of course, with the problem of Christian taboos, the no-nos of the Christian life that we encounter from place to place and from time to time. How much fellowship can you have with a Christian who lives in a different way than you do, who does things of which you do not approve?

The passage that discusses these questions of Christian ethics is a rather extensive one, which in itself indicates the size of the problem. The passage includes all of Romans 14, and runs through the first fourteen verses of chapter 15. It is very important to note that this whole section is part of an extended commentary of the apostle Paul on the command of Jesus to love one another. This has been the subject ever since the apostle turned to the practical part of this letter in Romans 12. There, you may remember, he tells us several things about love. First, the nature of love is to serve. We are given spiritual gifts so we might serve one another. Second, he tells us that love must be genuine, not "put-on."

Then in Romans 13 we learn that love must be submissive, especially to the powers that be, because they are put there by God. And in the latter part of chapter 13, Paul tells us that love must be universal; we owe love to everyone without exception.

Now in Romans 14 we learn that love must be patient and tolerant of other people's views. Think of someone whom you regard as perhaps less enlightened than yourself, and then read what Paul says to do to them.

> Accept him whose faith is weak, without passing judgment on disputable matters (v. 1).

That is very plain, isn't it? Do not reject him; do not ignore him; do not treat him as a second-class person. Accept him, but not for the purpose of arguing with him. Do not accept him in order to debate with him, but "without passing judgment on disputable matters."

Accepting without Correcting

Regardless of where you may struggle with other Christians and about what, you must realize that they are brothers and sisters in the family of God, if they are Christians at all. You did not make them part of the family—the Lord did. Therefore, you are to accept them because they are your brothers and sisters, and not with the idea of immediately straightening them out in their weak areas. That is a very necessary, practical admonition. Many of us love to argue and sometimes the first thing we want to do is straighten out the other person.

I remember a time years ago when I had finished preaching a message on a Sunday night, a man came up to me and said, "Let me ask you something. Do you believe that two Christians who love the Lord and are led by the Holy Spirit will read a passage of Scripture and both come out believing the same thing?" I said, "Yes, I think that sounds logical." "Well," he said, "can you explain why I believe the passage you preached on tonight teaches there will be no millennium, when you believe there is going to be one. What do you think of that?"

Being young and aggressive I said, "Well, I think it means that I believe the Bible and you do not." That immediately precipitated an argument and, with several other people gathered around, we went at it hammer and tongs for an hour or so.

Afterwards, I realized how wrong I was. I had to write to that brother and tell him I was sorry I had jumped on him like that. Of course, he had jumped on me, too, but that was his problem, not mine. I had to straighten out my problems, so I apologized to him and said, "I am sorry that I did not recognize the parts where we agree before we got on to those things over which we differ."

Paul wants us to understand that we are first of all to accept people, to let them know that we see them as a brother or a sister. Establish the boundaries of your relationship by some gesture or word of acceptance so they do not feel that you are attacking them. The Greek here indicates that we are not to accept people with an ulterior motive of arguing about our differences. The New English Bible phrases it, "without attempting to settle doubtful points." First, let there be a basic recognition that you belong to one another.

Paul goes on in verse 2 to more precisely define the areas of debate he has in mind:

One man's faith allows him to eat everything, but another man, whose faith is weak, eats only vegetables.

This is not dealing with nutrition, of course. In the early church there was a real moral question about eating meat. There were the Jewish restrictions against certain types of meat. Jews did not eat pork, and even beef and lamb had to be kosher; it had to be slain and processed in a certain way. So a Jew, or even one raised as a Jew, after he became a Christian always had great emotional difficulty in eating meat. I still wonder how the apostle Paul reacted when as a Christian he was first handed a ham sandwich!

There was also the problem in Rome and other pagan Greek and Roman cities relating to eating meat that had been offered to idols. Some Christians said that if you did that you were no different than the people who worshiped and believed in idols. But other Christians said, "Oh, no. How can that be? Meat is meat. The fact that someone else thinks of it as offered to idols does not mean that I have to think that way." In these pagan cities the best meat was sold in the butcher shop next to the temple. That is where the sacrifices were sold to the populace, who bought it and ate it without any question. So there was a difference of view in the church.

The Broad and Narrow Views

As in every such debate, there were two viewpoints. The liberal view was that it was perfectly all right to eat meat, whatever its source, and a stricter, narrower viewpoint held that it was wrong. It really does not make any difference what you are arguing about if it is in a debatable area, about which the Scriptures themselves do not speak. You will always hear these two opposing views. You can put many of our modern problems into this category. Should you drink wine and beer; should you go to the movies; should you dance; what about card-playing?

Let us be very clear that Scripture speaks about certain areas which are not debatable at all. It is *always* wrong to be drunk. It is *always* wrong to commit adultery or fornicate. In both the Old and New Testaments, God has spoken; he has judged these things. Christians are exhorted to rebuke and exhort and reprove one another—if necessary, even to discipline one another according to patterns set out in the Scriptures. This is not judging one another; the Word of God has judged, it has already pronounced what is wrong.

But there are other areas that are left open. The amazing thing to me is that Scripture always leaves those open. Paul will not give a "yes" or "no" answer about some of these things, because God does not do so. In other words, God wants to leave certain matters to the individual to decide. And, as we see later on, he expects that decision to be based upon a deep personal conviction.

It is clear here that Paul calls the liberal party "strong in the faith," but he regards the narrow party as being "weak in the faith." I do not agree with the New International Version in verse 1 where it reads, "Accept him whose faith is weak. . . ." This has nothing to do with the strength or weakness of the individual's faith. Paul is talking about someone who is weak in *the* faith. This is a doctrinal problem; he does not understand truth. Jesus himself said, "If you hold to my teaching, you are really my disciples. Then you will know the truth and the truth will set you free" (John 8:31,32).

Clearly, the mark of understanding truth is freedom, and Paul calls the person who understands truth one who is strong in the faith. Those who do not understand it clearly are weak in the faith. They do not understand the delivering character of truth.

William Barclay in his commentary on Romans has handled this well. He says:

> Such a man is weak in the faith for two reasons: (1) He has not yet discovered the meaning of Christian freedom; he is at heart still a legalist; he sees Christianity as a thing of rules and regulations. His whole aim is to govern his life by a series of laws and observances; he is indeed frightened of Christian freedom and Christian liberty. (2) He has not yet liberated himself from a belief in the efficacy of works. In his heart he believes that he can gain God's favor by doing certain things and abstaining from doing others. Basically he is still trying to earn a right relationship with God, and has not yet accepted the way of grace. He is still thinking of what he can do for God more than of what God has done for him.

The problem here is that of a Christian who is not yet understanding fully the freedom Christ has brought him, who
feels limited in his ability to use some of these things while
others feel free to do so. One is strong in the faith; the other
is called weak in the faith. Every church has these groups,
and Paul puts his finger precisely on the natural attitudes
we must avoid if we are going to accept one another. In
verse 3 he says,

> The man who eats everything must not look down on him who
> does not. . . .

The first thing is that the strong must not reject the one
who is still struggling, who is still weak. The word translated
"look down on" here really means "to push out." The strong
must not push him out: they must not exclude him. That
means they must not think about him in a disdainful or
contemptuous way.

Not Deliberate Weaklings

Some of us who feel we are free in certain of these areas
tend to regard those who are not yet free as weaklings,
which in some sense they are. But we are not to treat them
as if it is their own fault they are that way. It is wrong to
become offended when they do not behave as freely as we
think they should. Paul says, "The strong must not reject
the weak."

Someone has defined a legalist as someone who lives in
mortal terror that someone, somewhere, is enjoying himself.
But we must not think of legalists that way, because that is
not their motivation. We are not to exclude these people in
our contacts with one another. We must not form little
cliques within the church, or think of our group as being set
free while this group over here is very narrow. Paul actually
implies that if any of the so-called strong exclude weaker
brothers they have simply proved that they are just as weak
in the faith as the ones they have denied. Strength in the

faith means more than understanding truth. It means acting in a loving way with those who are weak. The truly strong in the faith will never put down those who are still struggling.

On the other hand, the apostle states in verse 3:

> . . . the man who does not eat everything must not condemn the man who does, for God has accepted him.

Here is the other side of it. Those who struggle must not look down on those who have freedom in these areas. Those who think it is morally wrong for a Christian to drink wine or beer must not look down on those who feel free to do so. They must not judge them. The word "condemn" means to sit in judgment, and it involves two things.

It involves, first, criticism or censoring. We are not to go up to people and say, "I do not see how you can be a Christian and do things like that." Their Christianity is established on grounds other than those. The word "condemn" also means categorizing people, classifying them as carnal Christians, reproving or rebuking them. In these areas we have no rights to reprove or rebuke. The church has no authority to impose behavioral standards or codes without the agreement of all who might be affected by them.

Sometimes there are good reasons for limitations, but they must be limitations which the individual makes for himself or accepts. They are not to be imposed upon him by others. What has happened often in the church is that those who are weak in the faith, who do not fully understand their freedom in Christ, are the majority party. They tend to make artificial standards for Christians and impose these standards on everyone who comes into the church. The implication is that you cannot really be a Christian unless you conform to these standards.

This has given rise to a tremendous distortion of Christianity in the eyes of the world. The world thinks that Christianity is a "don't" religion. This has happened widely in our day and for the most part, I think, the "narrow party" has

triumphed in evangelical churches. For this reason many
people will not touch the church with a fifty-foot pole, even
though they are fantastically interested in the gospel.

Now we come to the central part of this section. The
apostle sets forth three great facts, all supporting and explaining the great principle of acceptance.

Not My Brother's Changer

The first reason you must not look down on the weak and
judge or condemn the strong is that it is not your responsibility to change your brother in this area. He is not your
servant. This is what Paul says in verse 4:

> Who are you to judge someone else's servant? To his own
> master he stands or falls. And he will stand, for the Lord is
> able to make him stand.

This is very plain, is it not? The reason we are not to judge
each other is that we are not responsible for one another's
conduct in this area. Such responsibility is not defined in
the Scriptures. This is an open area that each one has to
decide for himself before God. The other person is not your
servant, Paul says; the Lord chose him. The Lord, then, is
the one responsible to change him. The Lord chose him
without asking you or me.

But Paul's point (verse 4) is that the man under consideration is being changed. He is on his way to standing. "He
will stand," Paul says. "Stand," of course, means that he
will be straightened out if he is doing wrong in any area. If
it is really wrong, God will straighten him out. I so much
enjoy that little pin that Bill Gothard gives out with the
letters P B P G I N F W M Y; that is, "Please be patient, God
is not finished with me yet."

We are all in the process of change. The Lord is doing it
and he will do it. He is changing us, and if we will just wait
a little while we can see some of the changes. If the problem
is one of not understanding truth, the solution is to teach
the truth more plainly. As people hear it and understand it,

they will be freed. To try to force them into reluctant compliance with something they do not yet understand is ridiculous and futile. Therefore, be patient. If they are being exposed to truth, they will change. Let the Lord change them; it is his responsibility. Not only will he do so, but he is perfectly able to do so. I like Phillips' translation here: "God is well able to transform men into servants who are satisfactory."

Now if the first point is that it is not your responsibility to change these people, the second one is that God is reading the heart and he sees something you cannot see about them:

> One man considers one day more sacred than another; another man considers every day alike. Each one should be fully convinced in his own mind. He who regards one day as special, does so to the Lord. He who eats meat, eats to the Lord, for he gives thanks to God; and he who abstains, does so to the Lord, and gives thanks to God. For none of us lives to himself alone and none of us dies to himself alone. If we live, we live to the Lord; and if we die, we die to the Lord. So, whether we live or die, we belong to the Lord (vv. 5-8).

That is an impressive point. Paul is saying that God can read hearts and you cannot. These distinctions and differences of viewpoint arise out of honest conviction which God sees even though you don't. Therefore, the individual is not simply being difficult because he does not agree with you. He is acting on the basis of what he feels is right, so give him the benefit of the doubt.

Believe that he is as intent on being real before God and true to him as you are, and if he feels able to indulge in some of these things you think are not right, then at least see him as doing so because he really feels that God is not displeased with him on that basis. Or, if he does feel limited and thinks he should not do certain things, do not get upset with him because he has not moved into freedom yet. Remember that he really feels that God would be displeased if he did those things; it is an honest conviction. The apostle makes clear here that every man should have that kind of conviction: "Let every man be fully persuaded in his own heart."

This means that you are not to act simply because you were brought up a certain way or because you *feel* it is right. Find some reason in the Scripture for it. Seek justification out of the Word of God. You may change your mind as your understanding of truth develops, but at least let it be on the ground of a conviction of the heart and mind.

Next Paul says that God sees both of these men and both of these viewpoints as honoring him. The one who thinks Sunday is a special day that ought to be kept distinct from all other days is doing so as unto the Lord. Therefore, honor and respect that viewpoint. On the other hand, someone may say, "No: when we are in Christ, days do not mean anything. They are not set aside for any special purpose. Therefore, I feel every day is alike, and I want to honor the Lord on every day." Do not be upset at that. He is expressing a deep conviction of his heart.

The one who drinks beer gives thanks to God for the refreshment of it and the taste of it, and that is perfectly proper. The one who says, "I cannot drink beer. I only drink coffee," gives thanks for the coffee. The coffee may do as much physical harm as the beer but, in either case, it is not a moral question. It is a question of what the heart is doing in the eyes of God. Sometimes we are too harsh with one another in these areas.

Some time ago I heard of a girl who was a converted nightclub singer. A fresh, new Christian, she was asked to sing at a church meeting. Wanting to do her very best for the Lord whom she had come to love, she dressed up the best way she knew how and sang a song that she thought was expressive of her faith. She did it in the "torchy" style of the nightclub singer. Someone came up to her afterwards and ripped into her. That person said, "How can you sing a song like that and claim to be a Christian? God could never be happy with a Christian who dresses the way you do, and sings in that kind of nightclub style." The poor girl stood

there for a minute and then, breaking into tears she turned
and ran.

That was a wrong and hurtful thing to do to her. Later on,
she might have changed her style, but God has the right to
change her, and no one else. Her heart was right, and God
saw her heart and honored it.

Liberty and Limitation

The last thing Paul says in this area is that our relationship with one another is more important than our life style:

> For none of us lives to himself alone and none of us dies to
> himself alone. If we live, we live to the Lord, and if we die,
> we die to the Lord. So, whether we live or die, we belong to
> the Lord (vv. 7,8).

Basically, what Paul is saying here is simply that living is
liberty and dying is limitation. In the context this is surely
what he means. He is not talking about funerals and life and
death in that sense. He is talking about those who feel free
to enjoy liberty to the fullest. They are living, while others,
because of deep convictions of their own, limit themselves,
and thus they are dying, because death is limitation.

"But whether we live," Paul says, "or whether we die, that
is not the important thing. The important thing is that we
belong to the Lord. He understands." Therefore, what we
ought to remember in our relationships with one another is
that we belong to the Lord. We are brothers and sisters; we
are not servants of each other. Since we are servants of the
Lord, he has the right to change us.

The third and final fact supporting this governing principle is that Christ alone has won the right to judge:

> For this very reason, Christ died and returned to life so that
> he might be the Lord of both the dead and the living. You,
> then, why do you judge your brother? Or why do you look
> down on your brother? For we will all stand before God's judg-
> ment seat. It is written:

> " 'As I live,' says the Lord,
> 'Every knee will bow before me;
>   every tongue will confess to God.' "

So then, each of us will give an account of himself to God. (vv. 9–12).

The Lord alone has the right to judge us in these areas and because he has been involved in both death and life, he has the ability to do so. He died, so he knows what ultimate and utter limitation is. He gave himself up to death, and he deliberately restricted himself in many things, so he knows what that is like. And he lives, so he is free to do anything and everything he desires; he knows what that is like. Therefore, he alone has won the right to judge us. He alone understands us.

So Paul says, "Stop trying to take his place. Stop trying to be Christ to the rest of the church or playing God to each other. You, the weak, why do you judge your brother? And you, the strong, why do you look down on your brother? It is wrong. You are trying to take Christ's place when you do that. But remember that all of us, men and women alike, all brothers and sisters together, must individually stand before God's judgment seat."

This is true in both a present and future sense. There is a sense in which we are before him all the time and we have to give an account to him and to him alone. But a day is also coming, as Paul mentions in 1 Corinthians 4, where he says, "The Lord returns and brings to light all the hidden things of the heart." All the things that we thought nobody ever saw will be brought to the light. We must then give an account to the Lord.

Again, Paul sums up everything in the first part: we are not servants of each other; we are brothers and sisters; we are all struggling; we are all in the process; we are all subject to change; we are all trying to understand truth more clearly as we go on; and we are all being freed by it. But in the process, the only one who has a right to do anything about it is the Lord. So we are to stop judging each other in these areas. Instead, we are to love one another and to show our love by accepting one another.

13

The Right to Yield

Continuing the lengthy passage dealing with matters of individual conscience—dietary restrictions, certain rituals, and so forth—Paul comes now to a discussion of what we can do about these matters; how we are to behave toward one another in these areas. The first thing we can do is given in verse 13 of chapter 14:

Therefore, let us stop passing judgment on one another. [That summarizes what we have covered so far: we are not to judge one another.] Instead, make up your mind not to put any stumbling block or obstacle in your brother's way.

I have always appreciated the fact that Scripture is never merely negative. It never says, "Do not do something," without suggesting a positive action to take its place. If all the apostle had to say was, "Stop judging," that would be like saying to someone, "Do not worry." If you try to stop worrying without any reason for doing so, you will find yourself worrying all the more. Scripture does not merely say, "Stop judging"; it says, "Stop judging others; if you want to judge, start with yourself." Are you pushing liberty so hard, insisting on your rights and your freedom so much that you are upsetting others and forcing them to act beyond their own

conscience? What you ought to judge is the effect your attitudes about some of these things have upon others.

The apostle goes on to give us two reasons why we must
not judge others, but must judge ourselves first in this area.
The first reason is in verse 14:

> As one who is in the Lord Jesus, I am fully convinced that no
> food is unclean in itself. But if anyone regards something as
> unclean, then for him it is unclean.

There is a fundamental, psychological insight into life here
that ought to govern our behavior in these areas. It is one
thing to be free yourself to partake of various things. You
may have arrived at that freedom by some direct teaching
of Scripture, even as Paul was taught by the Lord Jesus
himself. Actually, it does not really say in the Greek text, as
this version translates it, "As one who is in the Lord Jesus,"
that is, one speaking as a Christian. What Paul really says is,
"As one who has been taught by the Lord Jesus, no food is
unclean in itself."

It was the Lord Jesus who said, "No food is unclean." He
does not mean that all foods are good for you, for some
foods are not; some things you can eat are highly poisonous.
Jesus does not mean that everything is all right to take in;
he means that there is no moral question about food. Jesus
himself taught that, and Paul says, "That is enough for me.
That sets me free."

But that is not the only problem involved. The conscience
needs to be trained by this new insight into liberty. One
person's conscience may move much more slowly than another's; therefore, we are to adjust to one another's needs.

Crossing a Swinging Bridge

We can compare this to crossing a swinging bridge over a
mountain stream. Some people can run across a bridge like
that even though it does not have any handrails. They are
not concerned about the swaying of the bridge, or the danger of falling into the torrent below. But others are very

uncertain on such a bridge. They shake and tremble; they inch along. They may even get down on their hands and knees and crawl across. But they will make it if you just give them time, if you let them set their own speed. After a few crossings they begin to pick up courage, and eventually they are able to run right across.

It is like that with these moral questions. Some people cannot see themselves acting in a certain area that they have been brought up to think is wrong. As in the case of the swinging bridge, it would be cruel for someone who had the freedom to cross boldly to take the arm of someone who was timid and force him to run across. He might even lose his balance and fall off the bridge. This is what Paul is warning about in verse 15:

> If your brother is distressed because of what you eat, you are no longer acting in love. Do not by your eating destroy your brother for whom Christ died.

It is wrong to do that. It is not loving to force people to move at your pace. To refuse to indulge a freedom that you have for the sake of someone else; to adjust to his pace; is surely one of the clearest and truest exercises of Christian love.

Divisions over Minor Matters

The second thing Paul says in this regard is that the issue of freedom versus nonfreedom does not really demand unyielding firmness:

> Do not allow what you consider as good to be spoken of as evil. For the kingdom of God is not a matter of eating and drinking, but of righteousness, peace and joy in the Holy Spirit, because anyone who serves Christ in this way is pleasing to God and approved by men (vv. 16–18).

If you are going to create division by arguing so hard for your rights, or your freedom, or by flaunting your liberty in the face of those who do not agree with it, then you are distorting the gospel itself, Paul argues. He actually uses the word "blaspheme." You are causing that which is good, Paul says, the good news about Christ, to be blasphemed because you are making too much of an issue over a minor matter. You are making your rights so important that you have to divide the church over them, or separate from a brother or sister who does not believe as you do. In so doing you are saying to the watching world around that Christianity consists of whether you do, or do not do, a certain thing.

I once heard of a church that got into an unholy argument over whether they ought to have a Christmas tree at their Christmas program. Some thought a tree was fine; others thought it was a pagan practice. They became so angry at each other that they actually had fistfights over it. One group dragged the tree out, then the other group dragged it back in. They ended up suing each other in a court of law and, of course, the whole thing was in the newspapers for the entire community to read. What else could non-Christians conclude but that the gospel consists of whether you have a Christmas tree or not?

Paul says that is utterly wrong. The main point of the Christian faith is not eating or drinking or having Christmas trees. The main point is righteousness and peace and joy in the Holy Spirit. A non-Christian, looking at a Christian, ought to see these things; not wrangling and disputing and fighting and law courts, but righteousness.

You have seen that word, "righteousness," many times in Romans, and you know that it means God's gift of a sense of worth about yourself. Because of the death of Jesus on your behalf you are loved by him; you are accepted by him; you are a valuable person in his sight. In fact, he cheerfully and delightedly calls you his beloved child. That is righteousness, and from it, when we understand that, comes a sense of dignity and self-respect. The world ought to see you confident as to who you are, with a kind of underlying assurance that is without conceit. It will show that you have a basis of self-acceptance the world knows nothing about.

The second thing the world ought to see is peace. That

comes across visibly as a kind of calmness, an inner core of unflappability that is undisturbed by the minor irritations of the moment. It comes from a quiet assurance that God is present in the situation; that he will work it out for his glory, and therefore, we need not get upset or angry, or vindictive toward someone. It is hard for the world to get that impression of peace and calmness if they see two people screaming at one another over some issue. That does not look very calm.

God-Given Delight

The third element is joy. These three always go together: righteousness, peace, and joy; they are gifts of God. They do not come from you; they come from him. Joy is that delight in God that always finds life worthwhile, even though it may be filled with problems.

Joy in a Christian does not come from circumstances. I will never forget the time I met a lady who had been lying in her bed for thirteen years. Her arthritis was so bad that her joints were disconnected, and she could not even raise her hands. But the smile on her face was an outstanding witness to the fact that joy of this kind is a gift of God. It comes out of relationship, not out of circumstance. Because of that kind of joy, she had a tremendous ministry to the community around her.

Paul is saying that if you have that relationship, if it is the center of your focus and interest, then you can easily give up some momentary indulgence if it is going to bother someone or make him move beyond his own conscience. Sometimes, when you enter a main highway, you see a sign that says YIELD. That is what we are to do. The Christian philosophy is to yield, to give way. Do not insist on your rights under these circumstances.

In the second section, verses 19 to 21, Paul gives us some guidelines to follow:

> Let us therefore make every effort to do what leads to peace and to mutual edification. . . .

There are two guidelines set forth in verse 19. The first is in the phrase, "what leads to peace." Enjoy your liberties, indulge them wherever you desire, if you can do so without destroying someone else's peace. Enlarging on that idea, Paul goes on to say,

Do not destroy the work of God for the sake of food. . . .

Peace is the work of God. Nothing can produce lasting peace among people, especially those of different cultural backgrounds, except the work of God. It is the Spirit of God who produces peace. So, if for the sake of some right that you have, some liberty you feel, you destroy that peace, you are destroying what God has brought about. Do not do that; it is not worth the struggle.

The apostle's second guideline is that you stop exercising your liberty whenever it arrests someone else's learning process. All Christians ought to examine these issues more and more. They ought to investigate for new truth from the Word, constantly keeping an open mind on these matters. And they will, if we do not push them too hard. But if someone flaunts his liberty in such a way as to anger people and upset them, it will often harden them in their resistance to change, so that they no longer want to examine the question. That, Paul says, must be the limit to those who indulge in their liberty. Do not push people that far, or press them that hard. Rather, we are to help them understand the reason for our liberty.

Healthy Indulgence

I think it is a healthy thing for a Christian who has liberty in some of these areas to indulge it on occasion. The cause of Christ is never advanced by having every strong Christian in a congregation completely forego his right to enjoy some of these things. What happens then is that the question is settled on the basis of the most narrow and most prejudiced person in the congregation. Soon, the gospel itself becomes identified with that view. That is why the outside world often considers Christians to be narrow-minded people who have no concern except to prevent the enjoyment of the good gifts of life that God has given us.

It is a good thing for people to indulge their liberties. Such action raises questions in the minds of those who are not free, especially when they see that this indulgence is linked with a clear manifestation of righteousness and peace and joy in the Holy Spirit. It makes them think, when they see a godly person whom they admire and respect indulge freely in something that they have never been able to indulge in. Yet they cannot deny that he is a godly person. It is good for them thus to be forced to rethink their prejudices.

But Paul says to be careful, and judge how far you are going. If what you are doing upsets people and hardens them in their views so that they will no longer examine and investigate, then stop, you are going too far. That should be the limit. This is what the apostle means when he says, "All food is clean, but it is wrong for a man to eat anything that causes someone else to stumble. It is better not to eat meat or drink wine or do anything else that will cause your brother to fall."

Notice that Paul does not say it is wrong to make him think; it is never wrong to indulge your liberty to such a degree that your brother has to ask questions about his viewpoint. But it is wrong to persist in it to such a degree that you cause him to act beyond his convictions. That is causing him to fall.

Paul brings in the third guideline in verses 22 and 23:

> So whatever you believe about these things keep between yourself and God . . .

Unfortunately that translation suggests that you are to keep quiet about your liberties, but what he is saying is, if you have faith, have it between yourself and God. That is, let God and God's Word be the basis for your faith, and nothing

else. Be sure that what you are doing is not because of pride,
because you want to show off how free you are. You are
doing this because God has freed you by his Word. Paul
says if you do that,

> Blessed is the man who does not condemn himself by what he
> approves.

If you have really based your action on God's Word, then
your conscience will be free. You will not feel guilty and
troubled as to whether you are acting beyond what the
Word of God really says. You will be happy, free, blessed.
But,

> . . . the man who has doubts is condemned if he eats, be-
> cause his eating is not from faith; and everything that does
> not come from faith is sin (v. 23).

If you have not really settled this on the basis of Scripture,
but are acting only because you want to indulge yourself; if
you like this thing but you still feel a bit troubled by it, you
are going to be condemned by your conscience. And if you
are condemned by your conscience, you will feel guilty. And
if you act even though you feel guilty, you are not acting
out of faith and therefore, you are sinning. This is Paul's
argument.

"Without faith," Hebrews says, "it is impossible to please
God." Faith means believing what God has said. Thus, you
must base your actions in Christian liberty on what the
Word of God declares—not about any specific thing, but
upon the great principle of freedom which is set forth there.

To sum up, what Paul has said to us is this: *First,* do not
deliberately shock your brother or sister. Do not deliberately
do things that will offend them, or even make them feel uncomfortable. Think about them, not yourself.

Second: Give up your right when it threatens the peace or
hinders the growth of another individual. Be alert to judge
in that area.

And *third:* Never act from doubt. Act only from conviction, by the Word, and by the Spirit of God. If these problems are all settled on that basis, a congregation will be moving gradually toward the great liberty that we have as children of God.

What will happen in the eyes of the watching world? Christians will be seen to be free people, not controlled by scruples that limit them and narrow them in their enjoyment of God's great gifts. Nor will these things be of such importance that they are put at the heart and center of everything. The world will begin to see that the heart of the gospel is righteousness and peace and joy in the Holy Spirit, the gifts of God. Those gifts, then, are the basis for freedom in all these areas.

You are just as free to say "no" to the indulgence of a liberty as you are to say "yes" to it. That is true freedom. You are not free if you think you must have your rights. That is not freedom. Freedom is the right to give up your rights, for good and proper cause. That is what the watching world will see.

14

Our Great Example

In the fifteenth chapter of Romans Paul concludes his discussion of the different views on what is wrong and what is right for Christians. As an example of the continuing confusion over issues on which the Bible is silent, I just read that Dr. Carl McIntire, the flamboyant fundamentalist Presbyterian preacher, is now attacking Christians for going along with the change from Farhenheit to Celsius, or centigrade. He says it is nothing but a sneaky communist plot to take over the world—by degrees!

Paul summarizes his arguments thus far in the first two verses of chapter 15:

> We who are strong ought to bear with the failings of the weak, and not to please ourselves. Each of us should please his neighbor for his good, to build him up.

There are two thumbnail rules to follow when you have to make a quick decision as to whether you ought to insist on liberty in a certain area, or to give way to someone else's qualms. The first rule is: choose to please your neighbor rather than yourself. After all, this is what love does. Love does not insist on its own rights, Paul tells us in 1 Corinthians 13. Therefore, if you are loving in your approach, you

will adjust and adapt to others. I like J. B. Phillips' translation of this verse.

> We who have strong faith ought to shoulder the burden of
> the doubts and qualms of others, and not just to go our own
> sweet way.

The second rule, however, says to be careful that your giving
in does not allow your neighbor to be confirmed in his weakness. Do not leave him without encouragement to grow, or
to rethink his position. Please your neighbor, but for his own
good, always leaving something there to challenge his thinking, or make him reach out a bit, and possibly change his
viewpoint.

On a recent visit to Sacramento I talked with a man who
was a teacher in a Christian school there. He had been asked
by the school board to enforce a rule prohibiting students
from wearing their hair long. He did not agree with the rule,
so he found himself in a serious dilemma. If he did not enforce the rule the board had clearly indicated that he would
lose his job. If he did enforce it he would be upsetting the
students and their parents. Our culture has long since
changed from regarding long hair as a symbol of rebellion,
so this man found himself between a rock and a hard place.
His plea to me was, "What shall I do?"

My counsel was that we should not push our ideas of
liberty to the degree that they would upset the peace. I said
to him, "For the sake of peace, go along with the school
board and enforce the rule for this year. But make a strong
plea to the board to rethink their position and to change
their viewpoint. At the end of the year if they are unwilling
to do that, perhaps you might well consider moving to a
different place, or getting another position. That way you
would not be upsetting things, and creating a division or a
faction within the school."

Example from the Past

These kinds of decisions are not easy to make, but Paul is
saying to us that there are things we can do to work out

these problems. To encourage us in this, he gives us three
factors we can count on for help. The first one is the example
that comes to us from the past:

> For even Christ did not please himself but, as it is written:
> "The insults of those who insult you have fallen on me." For
> everything that was written in the past was written to teach
> us, so that through endurance and the encouragement of the
> Scriptures we might have hope (vv. 3,4).

The *first* example Paul gives us is Jesus himself. Even though
he was perfect Jesus ran into this kind of problem. Even
though he never on any occasion conducted himself in a way
that was in the slightest degree displeasing to God the
Father, nevertheless he encountered plenty of antagonism.
As Paul says, Jesus fulfilled the Scriptures which predicted
that those who did not like God's methods would take it
out on him. "The insults of those who insult you," he says,
"have fallen on me." And so our Lord had to bear with all
the unhappiness and even the insults of those who could
not be pleased even with what God himself was doing.

In Luke 14, for example, the Pharisees felt that Jesus was
not keeping the Sabbath properly. They were very upset
because he did things they felt were wrong to do on the
Sabbath. Now what did our Lord do? Did he give in to their
desire? No, he ignored their protest and did things that upset them even more. If he had gone along with their desires
they would never have learned what God intended the Sabbath to be. So the Lord did not adjust to their antagonism.

But on another occasion the Lord was accused of not paying his taxes. When the disciples told him about this he sent
Peter down to the lake to catch a fish, and in the fish's mouth
he would find a coin sufficient to pay the tax for both Peter
and himself. Jesus said he did this in order not to offend
them. That is, he adjusted to their complaint at that point.
If we think we have difficulty in applying these rules we
must remember that the Lord himself had difficulty.

There is still a third occasion when he publicly acknowledged that there was no way to please everyone: Jesus said,

"When John the Baptist came to you, he came neither eating nor drinking." That does not mean that John did not eat food: it means that he carefully observed certain dietary restrictions. He was probably a Nazarite who had taken a vow never to touch any kind of alcoholic beverage. So Jesus said, "When John came neither eating nor drinking, you said of him, 'He has a demon.' But when I came both eating and drinking, you called me a glutton and a drunkard. So how can I please you?" Jesus simply recognized the impossibility, at times, of adjusting to everyone. Thus he went ahead and did what God had sent him to do, and he let God take care of the difficulties.

I think this is what Paul has in mind here. He tells us that our Lord is the example, and there will be times when you cannot please anybody. There will be other times when you can—and if you can, you should. But there will be still other times when if you did, you would hinder people in their spiritual growth, and then you should not seek to please them.

Yielding Graciously

Not only do we have our Lord's life as our example, but the Old Testament also helps us here, especially in the matter of yielding up our rights. Remember when Abraham and Lot, his nephew, stood looking over the valley of the Jordan River? It was evident that they would have to divide the land between them. Abraham, who by right ought to have had the first choice, gave that choice to Lot. Lot chose the lush, beautiful, green areas of the Jordan valley, leaving Abraham the barren hills. So Abraham is an example of graciousness in that he gave up his rights.

Remember when Moses, according to the record, gave up his place as a prince in the household of Pharaoh? As Hebrews tells us, he gave it up in order that he might "suffer reproach with the people of God for a season." This is another striking example.

Remember David and Jonathan who were such close

friends? We see Jonathan gracefully yielding his right to
the throne to David, because he knew God had chosen him.
Jonathan also supported him against the wrath of his own
father. What a beautiful picture this is: Jonathan is willing
to give up so that David might gain.

When you come to the New Testament there is that scene
where John the Baptist says to Jesus, "He must increase; I
must decrease." And yet none of these men who gave up
ever lost anything. The point the apostle is making is that
these men gained by giving up. God was glorified, and they
themselves ultimately gained, because in giving up, they
achieved the objective that God was after.

Not only do we get help from the past, but Paul goes on
to show us that there is encouragement in the present as
well:

> May the God who gives endurance and encouragement give
> you a spirit of unity among yourselves as you follow Christ
> Jesus, so that with one heart and mouth you may glorify the
> God and Father of our Lord Jesus Christ (vv. 5,6).

There is no need to panic or to be afraid that we cannot
work out these problems, Paul says. God can drastically
change the situation. He is that kind of a God. The apostle
suggests two things we can do when we get involved in a
disagreement like this. First, there ought to be prayer,
prayer for unity. Paul himself prays that God may grant "a
spirit of unity among yourselves."

A Special Ministry of the Spirit

In Luke 11:13 Jesus said, "If you then, though you are
evil, know how to give good gifts to your children, how
much more will your Father in heaven give the Holy Spirit
to those who ask him!" Jesus is talking here about times in
your life when you need a special ministry from the Holy
Spirit who is already present. "If you know how to give good
gifts to your children, even though basically you have evil
in your nature, how much more willing is the heavenly Fa-

ther to give the Holy Spirit to you in times of problems and difficulties, to preserve the spirit of unity that you desperately need."

Recently I learned of a serious difference of viewpoint between two brothers in Christ. Not only did it bring them to a deadlock, but it affected a whole program God was putting together, one that depended upon their working together. It looked as though the whole thing would come to an ignoble end; nothing could be worked out. But others heard about this, and they and the two men involved began to pray, asking God to intervene. Then, at a final meeting scheduled to work this out one of the men said, "There is no need for us to talk about this, because God has already been talking to me. He showed me that I have been stubborn and obstinate about this, and I'm sorry. Let's go on to other things now; let's get the program started." The whole difficulty faded away because God is able to change situations and bring about unity. So prayer for unity is one of the most important things we can do when there is this kind of disagreement among us.

The second thing is to praise God for the relationship we already have, "so that with one heart and mouth you may glorify the God and Father of our Lord Jesus Christ." With one heart and mouth! Remember that you are brothers. Thank God together for what unites you and minimize the things that divide you. Remember the important thing is to manifest to a watching world the unity of brotherhood that God has brought about. In Ephesians 4 we are admonished to be "eager to maintain the unity of the Spirit in the bond of peace." Encouragement in the present, then, comes from prayer, asking God for the spirit of unity, and praising him for the unity that already exists.

We have had encouragement from the past, and encouragement from the present, and now Paul tells us to be encouraged by what the future holds:

Accept one another, then, just as Christ accepted you, in order to bring praise to God. For I tell you that Christ has become

a servant of the Jews on behalf of God's truth, to confirm the promises made to the patriarchs so that the Gentiles may glorify God for his mercy, as it is written:
"For this reason I will praise you among the Gentiles;
   I will sing hymns to your name" (Ps. 18:49).
Again, it says,
"Rejoice, O Gentiles, with his people" (Deut. 32:43).
And again,
"Praise the Lord, all you Gentiles,
   and sing praises to him, all you peoples" (Ps. 117:1).
And again Isaiah says,
"The root of Jesse will spring up,
   one who will arise to rule over the nations;
   the Gentiles will hope in him"
                                     (Rom. 15:7–12).

Paul is saying here that God is already working out a great program to reconcile the Jews and the Gentiles. God has announced that he is going to do it, and he will bring it to pass. In fact, the program has already stårted. It started when Christ accepted both Jews and Gentiles, regardless of the great differences between them.

Separated by Hate

In Paul's day the Jews held the Gentiles in contempt; they called them dogs and would have nothing to do with them. The Jews even thought it a sin to go into a Gentile's house, and they would never dream of eating with a Gentile. They regarded Gentiles with utter contempt. The Book of Acts tells us how Peter got into serious trouble with his Jewish friends because he went into the home of Cornelius the centurion and ate with him. It was only because Peter was able to show that the Holy Spirit had sent him there, and used him there, that he was able to justify his conduct to his friends.

Of course, if the Jews felt that way about the Gentiles, the Gentiles paid it right back in kind. They hated the Jews. They called them names; this is where modern anti-Semitism was born. Yet, Paul says, God is healing that kind of division by the work of Jesus.

And how did Jesus do it? Paul's point is that Jesus did his work by himself becoming a minister of circumcision. The New International Version says he "became a servant of the Jews." That is based on the idea that what Paul wrote was, "Christ became a minister of *the* circumcision," which is another name for the Jews. Actually what the text says is, "he became a minister of circumcision," which does not necessarily refer to the Jews as a people, but to their customs, rituals, and ceremonies.

The apostle is arguing that the Lord healed this breach between the Jews and the Gentiles by giving in and limiting his own liberty. He who designed the human body, he who made it perfect, exactly as it ought to be, consented to the act of circumcision. His body was mutilated. That part of his body which was the sign of the flesh was cut off. Jesus consented to that limitation and became a circumcized Jew. Further, he who declared in his ministry that all foods are clean, and thus gave clear evidence that he understood the liberty that God gives us in the matter of eating, never once ate anything but kosher food. He never had a ham sandwich, or bacon and eggs for breakfast.

Even further, he who was without sin insisted on a sinner's baptism. When he came to John, the Baptizer said, "Why are you coming to me? I need to be baptized by you. You do not need to be baptized." Jesus said, "Allow it to be so, for in this way it is fitting for us to fulfill all righteousness." So he who had no reason to be baptized nevertheless consented to be baptized.

Paul points out the results of that limitation: Jesus broke the back of the argument and contempt between the Jew and the Gentile. He reached both Jews and Gentiles to the glory of God. In the death and resurrection of Jesus, God showed his faithfulness to the Jews in fulfilling the promises made to the patriarchs. He also showed his mercy to the Gentiles, saving those who were without any promises at all. Thus the two, Jew and Gentile, shall fully become one, just as the Scriptures predict here. Paul gives quotations from the Psalms (the writings); from Deuteronomy (the Law);

and from Isaiah (the prophets), all of which agree that God can work out these kinds of problems.

Then Paul concludes with this magnificent benediction:

> May the God of hope fill you with great joy and peace as you trust in him, so that you may overflow with hope by the power of the Holy Spirit (v. 13).

What a magnificent verse! Whenever I am asked to give an autograph I almost always include this verse in it. Look how much you have going for you. All the great words of the Christian faith appear here: hope (twice, once it is called "overflowing hope"); and joy (great joy), and peace (calmness and confidence); and trust, (belief in a living God); and finally, the power of the Holy Spirit, (the invisible force that can open doors and no man shuts them, and can shut and no man opens—the power of God released among us).

I have been in places where the testimony of Christ in a community has been wrecked by the divisions and the attitudes of people toward one another in these areas. When we presume to write one another off because one has liberty we do not feel they should have; when we talk down to people and disparage those who do not have the faith and strength to act in liberty such as we do, we destroy the work of God.

The apostle is urging us to unite on the great positive words of our faith. We are to allow these qualities of hope, joy, peace, trust, and power to be visible when others see us gathered together as Christians.

It might almost be said that the letter to the Romans ends with this verse, Romans 15:13. Paul goes on, it is true, to give some personal words about his own ministry. But in a sense, the whole argument of this epistle is drawn to a close with this tremendous benediction:

> May the God of hope fill you with great joy and peace as you trust in him, so that you may overflow with hope by the power of the Holy Spirit.

How I hope these will be the characteristics that we manifest to the world around!

15

An Adequate Ministry

We are drawing to a close in our study of this great Epistle to the Romans. It closes just as it began, with a personal word from the apostle about himself, and about the church in Rome. There are two themes in the closing section of chapter 15: one is the church at Rome, and the other is the ministry of the apostle Paul. Concerning the church, the apostle begins:

> I myself am convinced, my brothers, that you yourselves are full of goodness, complete in knowledge and competent to instruct one another (v. 14).

You remember that the apostle began this letter by pointing out that the faith of these people was known around the world. Now in the fifteenth chapter, Paul gives us a further insight into this church. Here in verse 14 he says the church possessed three great qualities.

First: "I am convinced, my brothers, that you yourselves are full of goodness." That is, their motives were right. They had come to the place where they were motivated by a sense of goodness. This church at Rome was a responsive church, a compassionate church. It reached out to people in need, responding to those who had hurts and burdens.

No Theology Needed Here

The *second* thing the apostle says is that they were complete in knowledge. Now that is rather remarkable. Here was a church to which Paul did not need to give any new theology. Though Romans is one of the most deeply penetrating theological treatises in the New Testament, Paul did not write it because these people were doctrinally illiterate. They knew about the themes Paul emphasized in this letter, such as justification by faith—the gift of worth in God's sight. This gift could not be earned: it was a gift because of the work of Jesus Christ on their behalf. It was not earned by trying to do good works before God—this is impossible, and they understood that. They knew that though they did not deserve anything from God, nevertheless, they were his dearly loved children, and God accepted them fully.

They understood the nature of the flesh and the need for sanctification. Even though they had been redeemed, they knew they still possessed an old nature. The old Adam was still there, giving them trouble. Young Philip Melancthon, the colleague of Martin Luther, once wrote to Luther and said, "Old Adam is too strong for young Philip." These people at Rome understood this truth and they knew that this would be a lifelong struggle. Paul did not have to tell them this; they knew it before he wrote.

They knew also that God is working out a great plan, creating a wholly new humanity. Right in the midst of the ruins of the old he was producing a new man, and they knew they were part of it. They understood the great themes of glorification, and of the eternal ages to come. So Paul writes and says they were complete in knowledge.

The *third* thing the apostle had to say about this church was that they were competent to instruct one another. (This is where Dr. Jay Adams gets the title of his well-known book, *Competent to Counsel.*) What the apostle said was, "You are able to counsel one another." This remarkable truth is the answer to the terrible pressure often placed upon pastors who are expected to solve all the problems of their congregations, and to counsel everyone firsthand. That was never God's intention. The plan of God is that the whole congregation be involved in the work of counseling. The whole congregation is to be aware of what is going on with neighbors and friends and brothers and sisters, and do something about meeting their problems through the use of their spiritual gifts. So the church at Rome had the right motives, they had complete knowledge, and they had the full range of gifts, so that they were able to do many things within their church community and in the city of Rome.

But Paul also recognized that there were three things they lacked:

> I have written you quite boldly on some points, as if to remind you of them again, because of the grace God gave me to be a minister of Christ Jesus to the Gentiles with the priestly duty of proclaiming the gospel of God, so that the Gentiles might become an offering acceptable to God, sanctified by the Holy Spirit (vv. 15,16).

You would think a church that was theologically knowledgable, able to instruct and counsel one another in the deep problems of life, and filled with a spirit of goodness and compassion, would hardly need anything more said to them. Yet Paul wrote to such a church because they needed three other things.

Builtin Forgetfulness

First, they needed a bold reminder of the truth. "I have written you quite boldly on some points, to remind you of them again." I saw a man the other day, a grown man, with a string around his finger to remind him of something he wanted to be sure to remember. The fact that we so easily forget things is somehow built into our humanity. Surely one of the greatest proofs of the fall of man is that we have such a hard time remembering what we want to remember, yet we so easily remember what we want to forget!

We, too, need to be reminded again and again of these

172

great themes of the gospel. That is why in Romans 12 Paul says, "You need your mind renewed by the Holy Spirit." That is one reason Christians gather together in church meetings: we need to have our minds renewed. We need to be regularly called back to a vision of reality. Living out in the world, working every day among non-Christians, it is easy to be caught up by the attitudes of the world around us. It is easy to get the idea that life is designed to be a pleasant picnic, that we can rightfully work toward the day when we can retire and just enjoy ourselves. That attitude is prevalent everywhere, but that is not what the Bible says.

The Bible says we are in the midst of a battle, a battle to the death, against a keen and crafty foe. He wants to discourage us and defeat us, to make us feel angry and hostile. He knows how to do it and he never lets up. This life therefore is not designed to be a time of relaxing. There are times when we need recreation and vacations, when we can slow down a bit. But you never see the apostle Paul talking about quitting the battle. You cannot quit, as long as you are alive. So Paul tells us: We need to be reminded, day by day and week by week, that we are in a battle and that we have a crafty foe. This life is not all there is, by any means. This is school time, a training ground, where we are to learn our lessons. This life is preparing us for the real thing yet to come.

A Priestly Ministry

The *second* thing the apostle said the Christians at Rome needed was a priestly ministry. He told them, "You not only need to be reminded of the truth, but you need an example to follow. You need somebody you can see doing this kind of thing. That is what God has given me the privilege of doing. I have been called of God into this ministry, not only to be an example of leadership, but also to be like a priest working in the temple, to awaken among you a sense of worship, a sense of the greatness of God." We need this frequently. I know I do. From time to time I become dead inside, and I know you do, too. Despite all the exciting things happening, despite the tremendous encouragement on every side, there are times when we need to lift our eyes from our circumstances and stand before the greatness of God and see who it is we have to deal with, the One who is working through us. Paul did that and he is the example to us.

An Acceptable Offering

The *third* thing they needed, Paul says, is to "become an offering acceptable to God, sanctified by the Holy Spirit." Every congregation needs this. We need to labor, to pray, to work, to counsel, to evangelize. But all the activity of the Christian life is of no avail if it is not sanctified by the Holy Spirit, if it does not have in it that touch of God, that unction from on high, that divine wind blowing upon the dead bones and making them come to life. Paul is reminding the Roman Christians here of the ministry of prayer, and the need to remember that God himself must touch something—otherwise it is dead and useless. So Paul calls the church at Rome back to this tremendous reality. They had so much, but they needed this as well.

Now we have reached a fantastic passage, where, for the first time in this letter, we get a close look at this mighty apostle himself. Did you ever stop to ask yourself what influence the apostle Paul has had in your own life? He lived nearly two thousand years ago, and yet there is not one person among us who has not had his life drastically affected by this man. The whole course of history has been changed by the truths he taught. In fact, for the most part, history itself has been built around the letters, teachings, doctrine, and ministry of the apostle Paul. We would not even be here, for America as a nation would not exist, if this man had never lived. Even today we feel the freshness of his spirit, the greatness of his mind, and the fullness of his heart.

Paul tells us three things about his own ministry in this

last section: the principles that he worked under; the practice by which he carried them out; and finally, a word about the power that he relied upon:

> Therefore, I glory in Christ Jesus in my service to God. I will not venture to speak of anything except what Christ has accomplished through me in leading the Gentiles to obey God by which I have said and done—by the power of signs and miracles, through the power of the Spirit. So from Jerusalem all the way around to Illyricum, I have fully proclaimed the gospel of Christ. It has always been my ambition to preach the gospel where Christ was not known, so that I would not be building on someone else's foundation (vv. 17–20).

Concerning the principles of his ministry, Paul tells us four things. *First,* everywhere he went he found himself rejoicing. He said, "I rejoice, I glory in Christ Jesus, in my service to God." Why? Because when this man came into a city, he usually found it in the grip of Roman authority, ruled with an iron hand. He would find the people in widespread despair, empty and longing for something they could not find, fallen into degrading habits that were destroying homes and the very fabric of society itself. They were in the grip of superstitious fears. No church existed when he came, but after he had been there a while and had begun to preach these tremendous themes, light began to spring up in the darkness. People were changed; they began to live for the first time. They discovered why they were made, and excitement appeared in their lives. This made Paul rejoice for it happened everywhere he went.

What God Has Done

Second, Paul gives us the secret of this kind of ministry:

> I will not venture to speak of anything except what Christ has accomplished through me in leading the Gentiles to obey God by what I have said and done (v. 18).

That is the greatest secret God has to teach man—that man was designed, not to do something to make God happy, but

to let God work through the man. God would do the work
—that is what Paul said, ". . . Christ has accomplished
through me."

Not a week goes by but half a dozen posters and pam-
phlets cross my desk promoting the work of some man, telling me how much he has done for God. I have learned to
throw most of them into the wastebasket unopened. But you
never hear Paul telling how much he has done for God.
Everywhere it is how much God has done through him, and
that is the secret of a truly effective life.

It took the apostle ten years to learn that secret. Like
many young Christians, he started out with a great amount
of zeal and desire to turn the world upside down, and he
thought he had the equipment and gifts to do it. It took
God ten years to show him that his brilliant mind, his
mighty gifts, great personality, influence, and contacts were
of no value in the service of God. All God wanted was the
man himself; he would work through him. And when Paul
learned that secret, he launched upon this great ministry
that changed the history of the world.

Recently, a young man asked me, "Why did God punish
King David for numbering Israel?" That is one of the puz-
zles of the Old Testament. Why did God severely punish the
king and his people when he took a census of Israel? That
does not sound like a very serious crime, does it? But it
represented David's departure from the principle of dependence upon God to be his resource, and a shift to the
world's resource of numbers. Nothing has contributed more
to the weakness of the church than this dependence upon
numbers, as though a great crowd of people can do something. When you meet a man or a woman who is willing to
trust God to work through him/her, there is no limit to what
God can do. This is the secret of Paul's ministry.

Third, he tells us its manifestation, which is power; "by
the power of signs and miracles, through the power of the
Spirit" (v. 19). These signs and miracles were the signs of
an apostle. Paul tells us in 2 Corinthians that wherever he
went he performed signs and wonders. Many people ask

why we can't perform these signs today. The answer is that they were the mark of an apostle and only apostles did these things. Today we do not need any more apostles; we have the original ones, and their writings are available to us. What we do have is what Paul mentions, the power of the Spirit, and its impact on human lives.

The Corinthians once had the nerve to write Paul and say, "The next time you show up in Corinth, how about bringing a letter of recommendation from Peter and James and John?" Paul wrote back and said, "Do you mean that? Could you really mean that? Why, don't you understand that *you* are my letter of recommendation? Look at what's happened in your lives: You used to be drunkards and homosexuals and thieves and murderers—'such were some of you!' But what are you now? Look at the change! You are all the letter of recommendation I need." Paul's life and ministry were constantly characterized by the display of the power of God to change lives.

Then *finally*, look at how widespread his ministry was:

> So from Jerusalem all the way around to Illyricum, I have fully proclaimed the gospel of Christ (v. 19).

You really must have a map to see that. Jerusalem is way down on the eastern corner of the Mediterranean Sea, in Asia. Paul had traveled up and down that coast, on into what we call Turkey, in Asia Minor, up across the Dardanelles into Europe, then into Macedonia and Greece. He had gone, as he tells us here, into Illyricum, now called Yugoslavia. The nature of his ministry was pioneering:

> It has always been my ambition to preach the gospel where Christ was not known (v. 20).

He never wanted to build on another man's work. I believe this is characteristic of the Spirit of God. He loves to thrust out into new areas. (Did you ever notice that the word for news, as in good news, is made up of the first letters of north, east, west, and south?) We are to reach out with the good news, as Paul did.

Planning Perspective

Now for a paragraph on how he practiced this ministry:

This is why I have often been hindered from coming to you. But now that there is no more place for me to work in these regions, and since I have been longing for many years to see you, I plan to do so when I go to Spain. I hope to visit you while passing through and to have you assist me on my journey there, after I have enjoyed your company for a while (vv. 22–24).

There is Paul's word about how practical his ministry was. He tells us *first*, that it involved planning for the future. I am always running into Christians who think that God gives his orders directly to them while they are moving. They think of the Christian life as going on automatic pilot where they just float around, waiting for orders as they go. They never think of planning or looking ahead. But Paul did not live like that.

For many years he had longed to go to Spain, and he planned to do so. But notice something about his planning. First, it was flexible; he did not have a timetable. He went according to the way God opened the doors, but he planned to go in a certain direction, which he kept clearly in mind. He did not tell God how or when it had to be. That is Christian planning.

Second, he was persistent; he did not give up. He had set his heart on Rome and Spain, and that is where he was going. It did not matter how long it took, he kept plodding steadily toward that goal. There is no record that Paul ever got to Spain although there are some hints in Scripture that he undertook a fourth missionary journey after he wrote the letters to Timothy. In any event, Spain was the focus of his heart's desire.

The *third* thing about Paul's planning was that it always involved a team. He never went alone, and he says to these Romans, "When I come to Rome, I expect you to help me to go on"—perhaps to supply some assistance, some money, and to pray as he went. Paul never worked independently, as a prima donna; he always involved others.

The second factor about his ministry is found in verse 25 and following:

> Now, however, I am on my way to Jerusalem in the service of the saints there. For Macedonia and Achaia [Greece] were pleased to make a contribution for the poor among the saints in Jerusalem. They were pleased to do it, and indeed they owe it to them. For if the Gentiles have shared in the Jews' spiritual blessing, they owe it to the Jews to share with them their material blessings. So after I have completed this task and have made sure that they received this fruit, I will go to Spain and visit you on the way. I know that when I come to you, I will come in the full measure of the blessing of Christ (vv. 25–29).

Now, not only was Paul practical in that he planned, but also he fulfilled past commitments. Some Christians, I find, are forever jumping into new things before finishing the old. But Paul did not do that. Many years before this, in the council at Jerusalem (Acts 15), Paul and Barnabas were sent to Antioch with a letter to the church, settling the question of circumcision for the Gentiles. In that letter, Paul was specifically asked to be careful to remember the poor. Now, many years later, he is fulfilling that requirement. He has taken up an offering every place he has gone, and now he wants to deliver it personally to the famine-stricken saints in Jerusalem and Judea. Notice that it is not beneath the apostle to give material help. He is not going up there to preach to these people, but to help them with material things. Christianity involves both emphases—spiritual and physical. Paul was willing to take up offerings and personally carry the money to those in need. But here he gives us the principle of sharing:

> . . . for if the Gentiles have shared in the Jews' spiritual blessings, they owe it to the Jews to share with them their material blessings (v. 27).

If someone blesses you spiritually, and the only way you can thank him is with material things, then do it, Paul says.

That is God's program, to give back in material things for
the spiritual blessings you have received. Notice it says,
"After I have completed this task. . . ." He is not going
to quit until he is through. He will wrap it up well and do
it right. "When I have made sure that they have received
this fruit, then I will go to Spain and visit you on the way."

The third aspect of the practical character of Paul's ministry is his trust in the power of God:

> I know that when I come to you, I will come in the full
> measure of the blessing of Christ (v. 29).

He counted on God to come through. That introduces the
last paragraph, where he touches on the power of his
ministry:

> I urge you, brothers, by our Lord Jesus Christ and by the love
> of the Spirit, to join me in my struggle by praying to God for
> me. Pray that I may be rescued from the unbelievers in Judea
> and that my service in Jerusalem may be acceptable to the
> saints there. Then by God's will I can come to you with joy
> and together with you be refreshed. The God of peace be with
> you all. Amen (vv. 30–33).

What was behind this mighty apostle's ministry? Why has
it lasted for two thousand years? What was it that opened
the doors and gave him access even into Caesar's household,
and before the throne of the emperor himself? Paul would
tell you it was the prayers of God's people for him. He was
well aware of the power of prayer, and he urges them to
pray.

To Honor the Lord Jesus

Here we have a brief word on the nature of prayer. What
is the basis of it? "I urge you, brothers, by our Lord Jesus
Christ and by the love of the Spirit. . . ." Prayer is born of
the Spirit of God within us, awakening a desire to help, a
sense of love and compassion. And the reason we pray is to

honor the Lord Jesus. When people see that the honor of
Christ is involved, and the love of the Spirit is fulfilled by
prayer, they will really begin to pray. Paul says, "Join me
in my struggle." Life is a struggle, and Paul sees prayer as
a way of fighting in that combat. It is a great weapon which
can batter down some doors and open others. It can remove
obstacles, withstand tremendous pressure and forces, and
uphold and sustain people.

Notice what Paul requested of his readers: "Pray for pro-
tection from the unbelievers, and for acceptance from the
saints." These are the two areas that Satan loves to attack.
If he can lay a person low with physical illness, or spiritual
attack, he will do so. Prayer is particularly powerful at this
point; it can protect someone in danger. When Paul arrived
in Jerusalem, as we learn from the Book of Acts, there came
a moment when he was set upon by a mob in the temple
courts. They were out to kill him, right on the spot. They
had rocks in their hands and were going to stone him to
death. But it just so happened that at the critical moment,
the commander of the Roman legion on the other side of
the wall, in the castle of Antonia, looked over into the
temple court and saw what was going on. He came down
with a band of soldiers and rescued the apostle in the nick
of time. So prayer was answered, and Paul was protected
from the unbelievers.

Earlier in Acts, Luke tells us, when Paul came with his
gift, there were many Christians in Jerusalem of Jewish
background who did not want to accept Paul. They regarded him as a renegade, a traitor to the Jewish cause.
They were turning their backs on him. But James, in answer
to prayer, interfered. He asked Paul to show that he was not
an enemy of the law, and to take on a certain commitment
to demonstrate to the people that he was not against the
law. That turned the tide, and Paul's ministry was accepted.
Thus Paul's prayer requests were honored and God gave
him what they asked.

Finally, Paul gives us his personal expectation of the results of their prayers:

Then by God's will I can come to you with joy and together with you be refreshed (v. 32).

The Book of Acts closes three years from this time, with the apostle Paul finally arriving in Rome, after being shipwrecked, and after arduous travels. On his way to the capital city Paul was met by a delegation of Christians from the church of Rome. There in a place called the Three Taverns, they sat down and had fellowship and refreshment together. What an encouragement it was to the apostle's heart that these Christians were able to come out and meet him. He was coming as a prisoner chained to a Roman guard, on trial for his life, and sentenced to appear before the emperor. But they encouraged his heart and refreshed his spirit.

I hope this review of Paul's ministry will remind you that we are in a battle and we cannot take time out. We have to maintain the task and be faithful to what God has called us to do. Above everything else, we must seek the mighty unction of the Holy Spirit on all that happens. It must not be just a mechanical process, but the power of God released among us.

16

All in the Family

Many people ignore Romans 16 because they see in it nothing but a list of names of people long since dead and gone. But in many ways this is one of the most exciting chapters in Romans, as I think you will see.

Something in all of us wants to see our names preserved. Years ago I visited the Natural Bridge of Virginia. There were hundreds of names and initials scratched on the rocks, but high up on the side of it, above almost every other name, was scratched "George Washington." Even the father of our country felt the urge to gain a kind of immortality by carving his name on the rock.

But here in Romans 16 is a list of names of men and women who never knew they were going to be famous. Probably if they had known that a mention in one of Paul's letters was to give them undying fame there would have been a long line of people outside his door urging him to include them in the letter. But these names are mentioned only because they were personal friends of Paul's in Rome, or they were with him in the city of Corinth where the letter was written.

In the first twenty-four verses, thirty-three names are mentioned. Nine of these people were with Paul—eight men

and one woman. There are twenty-four names of people
who were in Rome—seventeen men and seven women. There
are two households mentioned, and two unnamed women—
the mother of Rufus and the sister of Nereus—as well as
some unnamed brethren. So there is quite a list of people
the apostle knew personally in Rome though he himself had
not yet visited that city. These are people he had known
somewhere else in the Roman Empire. We tend to think of
these ancient days as a time of limited travel, and they were.
It took weeks to reach cities that we now reach in less than
an hour by plane. Nevertheless, these people got around,
and here is a confirmation of that fact.

This passage has three simple divisions: first, Paul's greetings to the brothers and sisters at Rome (the first 16 verses);
then a brief warning about phony Christians who were there
in Rome; and finally, greetings from the brothers who were
with Paul as he wrote. The letter to the Romans was carried by a traveling businesswoman, Phoebe, who is intro-
duced to us in the opening verses of this chapter:

> I commend to you our sister Phoebe, a servant of the church
> in Cenchreae. I ask you to receive her in the Lord in a way
> worthy of the saints and to give her any help she may need
> from you, for she has been a great help to many people, in-
> cluding me (vv. 1,2).

The whole church can be grateful to this woman for her
faithfulness. She bore and preserved this letter throughout
that hazardous journey from Corinth to Rome. She is called
by the apostle "a servant of the church in Cenchreae."
Cenchreae was a port of Corinth, located about nine miles
east of the city. Evidently a Christian church had grown up
there, and Phoebe was a deacon in it. (That is really the
term, not "deaconess," as the King James version puts it.
That is a sexist term; the word is the same for male or
female.) That does not mean she held some governmental
office in that church, however. We sometimes read present-
day meanings into these words. It means that she had as-
sumed a ministry on behalf of the church. She represented

them in some labor, and whether it was material, physical, or spiritual, she was faithful in it. So Paul commends her to these Christians in Rome and asks them not only to receive her but to help her, "She has been a help to many others," he says, "and to me."

You cannot read Romans 16 without being impressed by the number of women Paul mentions—many more than in any other literature of that day. Women occupy a prominent place in these letters of the New Testament. They handled important tasks within the church, according to the gifts they had. There is strong suggestion here that Phoebe was a teacher or an evangelist—a laborer for the gospel with Paul. We do not know much more about her, but her name has been preserved forever because of this mention.

A Church in Their Home

Paul now turns to greet those he knew in Rome, and he begins with a very well-known husband and wife team:

> Greet Priscilla and Aquila, my fellow workers in Christ Jesus.
> They risked their lives for me. Not only I but all the churches
> of the Gentiles are grateful to them.
> Greet also the church that meets at their house (vv. 3,4).

We see this couple first in Acts 18, where Luke tells us they were Jews, tentmakers by trade, who were driven out of Rome by the decree of the Emperor Claudius. (That is a historical mention, dated in 52 A.D.) They went to Corinth, took up their trade there, and met this strange young Jew, also a tentmaker, who had come from the north. Saul of Tarsus apparently moved in with them and soon led them to Christ. Theirs was probably the first home in Corinth to hold a church. Luke tells us that after two years there, Paul left to go to the great city of Ephesus, and Priscilla and Aquila went with him. Again, they took up the trade of tentmaking and again opened up a church in their home.

They also ministered in the synagogue in Ephesus, for Luke tells us that one morning they heard a mighty and eloquent man named Apollos preaching. But it was evident to them that he did not understand the fullness of the gospel for he preached only what John the Baptist taught, that "One was coming, who would do mighty things." After the service they invited him home to dinner (that is a wonderful thing to do for a preacher!) and instructed him more fully. Because of their service to him Apollos went on to Corinth where he had a mighty ministry in the Word of God. Incidentally, of the six times their names are mentioned, four times Priscilla's name is put first—which indicates that she had the gift of teaching rather than her husband.

Now they are in Rome, having traveled from Corinth and Ephesus. Paul greets them, and reminds the church that they had risked their lives for him. That was probably in the uproar that broke out in the city of Ephesus, recorded in the latter part of Acts, when the whole city was upset and a mob was intent on taking Paul's life. He reveals the fact that everywhere this couple went they had a church in their home.

In these early days Christians did not meet in buildings like we have now. In fact, for 300 years there is no mention of church buildings in church history. What a relief, not to be bothered with a church building program! People got together where they could for larger meetings. But here in Rome there were at least three (and probably many more) house churches where Christians gathered, one of which was in the home of Priscilla and Aquila.

Paul goes on to mention two other friends:

> Greet my dear friend Epaenetus, who was the first convert to Christ in the province of Asia.
> Greet Mary, who worked very hard for you (vv. 5,6).

Epaenetus was never forgotten, for he was the first one to believe the gospel when Paul came to the province of Asia, of which Ephesus was the capital. You never forget the first one you lead to Christ. No matter how many others follow, you never forget the first fruits. We do not know what Epaenetus was doing in Rome but he was cherished because he was the first to exercise faith in Asia. Associated with him is Mary, whom Paul calls "Mary the toiler." She is one of the group of unknown women in the Gospels who had the gift of helps. She could not teach or preach or evangelize, but she could work, and she did. Paul is very careful to remember these women and men who had the gift of helps.

Friends and Relatives

Then he mentions some relatives and friends:

> Greet Andronicus and Junias, my relatives who have been in prison with me. They are outstanding among the apostles, and they were in Christ before I was.
> Greet Ampliatus, whom I love in the Lord.
> Greet Urbanus, our fellow worker in Christ, and my dear friend Stachys.
> Greet Apelles, tested and approved in Christ (vv. 7–10).

Andronicus and Junias were relatives of Paul, and since he says they were "in Christ before me," this takes us back to the very first days of the church, back to the ministry of Stephen in Jerusalem. What it must have meant to the young Saul of Tarsus, who was breathing forth threatenings and slaughter against the Christians there, to learn that two of his own kinsmen had become Christians! Undoubtedly the prayers of Andronicus and Junias affected the apostle.

It is hard to tell whether this is a husband and wife team, or two brothers. It all depends on the name "Junias." If it is "Junias" with an "s," as we have it here, it is a male; if it is "Junia," as the King James Version has it, it is female. But whoever they were, they were Jews, relatives of Paul, who had become Christians. There is a wistful note here as Paul remembers that they were in Christ before him, and no doubt were praying for him. Somewhere along the line they shared a prison term with him. There is no better place to make friends than in jail. You have to get to know your fellow-inmates—there is no escaping them! They became fast friends, as well as relatives, and Paul speaks highly of them. He says that even the twelve apostles in Jerusalem held them in high regard. What they were doing in Rome we do not know—doubtless they were leaders in the church there.

Ampliatus is an interesting name. In the cemetery of Domitilla, among the catacombs in Rome, there is a highly decorated tomb with the single name "Ampliatus" written on it. A single name like this implies that the man was a slave, but as the tomb is rather ornate, it indicates that he was a Christian and highly respected by the leaders in Rome. We cannot be sure that it was the same person Paul mentions here, but most likely it is. Therefore this man, though a slave, had a great ministry among the brethren in Rome.

We know no more about Urbanus and Stachys than what Paul mentions here. Somewhere, Urbanus joined Paul's team, and also "his dear friend Stachys," and that is all we know. But I have always been fascinated by this man Apelles, whom Paul says has been "tested and approved in Christ." (I would love to have that inscription on my tombstone!) This man will forever be known as one who endured a testing of his faith and who stood against the pressure. Thus he has been approved in Christ. His name means "called," and he certainly proved himself to be one whom God had called.

Christians in High Places

In the latter part of verse 10 and in verse 11 two groups are mentioned, involving Christians and perhaps non-Christians as well.

> Greet those who belong to the household of Aristobulus.
> Greet Herodion, my relative.
> Greet those in the household of Narcissus who are in the Lord.

Dr. William Barclay, probably the best commentator of all in getting at the background of biblical stories, tells us that

Aristobulus may have been the grandson of King Herod the
Great, who lived in Rome. He was behind the scenes politi-
cally, but was the close friend of the Emperor Claudius.
When Aristobulus died, his household, that is, his servants
and slaves, became the property of the emperor but it was
still known as the household of Aristobulus. It is this group,
probably, that Paul is referring to. If so, it means that even
in the royal household there were a number of Christian
servants and slaves who exercised great influence on the
leaders of Rome—even the emperor himself. This is supported, I think, by the fact that Paul mentions his relative,
Herodion, in connection with these servants. You can see
from his name that this man had connection with the family
of Herod. This is also a hint to us that Paul himself had
some connection with the ruling family of the Jews. His
relative, Herodion, had become a Christian, and was living
there in Rome as part of the household of either Aristobulus
or Narcissus.

The most famous Narcissus we know in Roman history
was a former slave who became the personal secretary of the
Emperor Claudius. He gained much wealth, because he was
in charge of the emperor's correspondence, and his palm
had to be greased before a letter could get through to the
emperor. When Claudius was murdered, Nero took over,
and he also took over the household of Narcissus. Shortly
after Nero came to the throne he forced Narcissus to commit suicide, as he did many other men. But it is very clear
from this mention here that there were Christians among
his household. "Greet those in the household of Narcissus
who are in the Lord." Already, in the heart of the Roman
Empire, a Christian witness had been established.

Next, we get another band of hard-working ladies:

Greet Tryphaena and Tryphosa [I have always enjoyed those
names!] those women who work hard in the Lord.
Greet my dear friend Persis, another woman who has worked
very hard in the Lord.
Greet Rufus, chosen in the Lord, and his mother, who has been
a mother to me, too (vv. 12,13).

These words of Paul's open up hidden vistas and bring the whole flavor and color of this first-century Christian life home to us. Here were Tryphaena and Tryphosa, these dear maiden sisters who worked very hard. We do not know what they did, but there is a delicate irony here. When Paul wrote this he probably smiled to himself, for their names mean "dainty" and "delicate"—yet they were hard workers. Their names suggest nobility, and perhaps they were born to aristocracy. And yet, they who did not have to work for a livelihood worked hard in the service of the Lord.

We know nothing about Paul's dear friend Persis, other than that she, too, had worked with him somewhere, perhaps traveling in his company of evangelists. In verse 13 we have Rufus, chosen in the Lord, and his mother, who had been a mother to the apostle, too. There seems to be little doubt that Rufus, along with his brother Alexander (mentioned in the Gospel of Mark), were the sons of Simon of Cyrene. In the gospels we are told that as our Lord was making his way down the Via Dolorosa in Jerusalem on his way to the cross, he was so weak from loss of blood that he tripped and fell. The Roman soldiers laid hold of a passing stranger whom they compelled to bear the cross to Calvary. That man was Simon of Cyrene, a Jew coming into the city for the Passover. His home was in North Africa, and he evidently had little or no interest in the things of Christ until he was forced to carry the cross of Jesus. Though we do not know the details it is evident that this man became a Christian and there is a hint in the Book of Acts that he was present on the day of Pentecost.

His two sons, Alexander and Rufus, became outstanding men in the Christian community. There is an Alexander who comes to the rescue of Paul in the city of Ephesus, at the time of the outcry there. There is a Rufus here in Rome, who is well known, and Paul sends his greetings to him, and reminds him also that Rufus' mother had been his mother, too, at some time. Back in the earliest days of the gospel ministry young Saul of Tarsus, coming to Jerusalem to sit at the feet of Gamaliel the great Jewish teacher, had

probably stayed in the home of Simon of Cyrene and his
two sons, Alexander and Rufus. Later they became Christians, and Paul cherished them as friends he had known
even before his own Christian days.

Then in verse 14 we find a businessmen's group:

> Greet Asyncritus, Phlegon, Hermes, Patrobas, Hermas and the
> brothers with them.

Here, possibly, is a kind of male commune, all with Greek
names. These may have been young businessmen who had
come to Rome and formed a house church in their bachelors'
quarters there. Paul sends his greetings to them and all
the brothers with them.

Then a final group, perhaps another house church in
Rome:

> Greet Philologus, Julia, Nereus and his sister, and Olympas
> and all the saints with them.
> Greet one another with a holy kiss.
> All the churches of Christ send greetings (vv. 15,16).

Philologus means "a lover of the word," and this was probably a nickname given to him, just as Barnabas was called
"the son of consolation," even though that was not his name.
Here was a man who loved the Word of God, and gathered
with him these men and women—Julia, Nereus and his
sister.

Nereus is another fascinating name. Dr. Barclay suggests
that he may have been the housekeeper of a prominent
Roman citizen named Flavius Clemens, later to become
Consul of Rome, the highest political office in the city, who,
in 95 A.D., was condemned to death by the Emperor Domi-
tian because he was a Christian. His wife, Domatilla, also
a Christian, was banished by the emperor. We can see from
these names that Roman society had already been infiltrated
by the gospel before Paul ever arrived in the city. That is
why, at the beginning of this letter, he says, "Your faith is
being reported all over the world." These prominent Chris-

tians had already penetrated society from top to bottom. That is the way Christianity should work. I do not think it makes its best progress by massive campaigns. It makes its best progress when it infiltrates all levels of society and brings them together in the church of Christ.

Divisive Forces

Now we have a warning paragraph, indicating that Paul is thinking of his own trip to Jerusalem and the threat that awaits him from the Judaizers there:

> I urge you, brothers, to watch out for those who cause divisions and put obstacles in your way, contrary to the teaching you have learned. Keep away from them. For such people are not serving our Lord Christ, but their own appetites. By smooth talk and flattery they deceive the minds of naive people. Everyone has heard about your obedience, so I am full of joy over you; but I want you to be wise about what is good, and innocent about what is evil.
>
> The God of peace will soon crush Satan under your feet. The grace of our Lord Jesus be with you (vv. 17–20).

This is a very helpful passage on what to do about problems within the church. Here is a group of people who are professing Christians, but who, to judge by the apostle's language, are not truly believers. The danger, as Paul outlines it, is that they create factions within a church—that is, little dissident groups that gather about and emphasize one particular point of doctrine or teaching, to the exclusion of everything else. That is always a problem within the church when people think one particular thing is most important. We have people today who emphasize tongues, or prophecy, or some phase of teaching that they think is the mark of a true believer, to the exclusion of everything else. Paul warns about this.

The second thing they do is to introduce practices or ceremonies that Paul calls "obstacles to faith," certain rituals or practices that these groups insist are the marks of true Christianity. They build a sense of superiority in their

devotees. They say, "If you have this mark, then you really
are a Christian." Their motives, Paul says, are not to serve
Christ, even though they say they do. These factions are
really out to advance themselves, to get a following, to gain
prestige. You can tell what they want by the way they act.
Their methods are to come on with smooth and plausible
talk. They always use scriptural language, and appear to be
the most dedicated and devoted of believers. Have you
noticed how many of the cults today are trying to go back
to the Scriptures, arguing from them a groundwork for their
faith?

Another method is flattery. They make Christians feel important. They lift them up above the rest and give them a
peculiar mark of distinction, and flatter their egos as being
members of the "true" church. Such methods always cause
division. When some group like this appears many tend to
want to rush in and excommunicate them, read them out of
the church from the pulpit, or violently attack them. Paul
does not say to do any of those things. His advice is to keep
away from them. Ignore them! "You Christians in Rome have
a reputation for obedience. You have a spirit of wanting to
obey what the Lord says. Now here is your word from the
Lord: Do not follow them. Do not get involved with these
separatist groups. The God of peace, who will preserve the
peace of the church, will also crush Satan under your feet."
If you keep away from them something will happen to open
the eyes of people to the unscriptural position of these
groups, and they will lose their following. The peace will be
preserved without a lot of warfare and dissension.

In verses 21–23 we have the greetings of those who are
with Paul in Corinth:

> Timothy, my fellow worker, sends his greetings to you, as do
> Lucius, Jason and Sosipater, my relatives.
> I, Tertius, who wrote down this letter, greet you in the Lord.
> Gaius, whose hospitality I and the whole church here enjoy,
> sends you his greetings.
> Erastus, who is the city's director of public works, and our
> brother Quartus send you his greetings.

This brings us to the final paragraph when, as was his custom, Paul takes his pen and writes the last words himself. Up to this point he has been dictating this letter to a man who identifies himself in verse 22: "I, Tertius, who wrote down this letter, greet you in the Lord." The apostle must have said something to him, such as, "Tertius, you've written this whole thing and you must have writer's cramp by now. Just write another line and send your own greetings." The name indicates that he was a slave, because his name means "Third." In slave families they did not bother to think up names; they just numbered the children. First, Second, Third, Fourth, Fifth, and so on. Here are Third and Fourth of a family of slaves. (His brother Quartus, Fourth, is mentioned in verse 23.) They are educated slaves who have become Christians. These men can read and write, and are part of this group in Corinth.

You can picture them gathered in the home of Gaius, the gracious, genial, generous host of the city, who is also mentioned in Paul's first letter to the Corinthians. Gaius opened his house to the entire Christian community. So here is Paul, sitting with his friends. Tertius is writing down the letter, and the others are gathered around listening to Paul as he dictates, profiting much from the writing of these great truths. With Paul is his dear son in the faith, Timothy, whom we know so well from the two letters addressed to him. Paul spoke of him always in the highest terms: his beloved son in the faith, who had stayed with him so long and remained faithful to the end. The very last letter Paul wrote from his prison cell in Rome was to Timothy.

Paul also mentions Lucius, Jason, and Sosipater, his relatives. Here in Romans 16 are mentioned six members of Paul's family, kinsmen who are now Christians. Some were Christians before him, but some Paul influenced toward Christ. They come from various places. Lucius appears to be the same one who comes from Cyrene, mentioned in chapter 13 of Acts as one of the teachers in the city of Antioch. Jason was evidently Paul's host when the apostle went to the city of Thessalonica, in Macedonia. Paul stayed in Jason's home when a riot broke out in the city. Sosipater may be the man from Beroea, mentioned in Acts 20 as Sopater, whom Paul met in Macedonia and accompanied to Jerusalem with the offering to the churches there.

The final name is Erastus, director of public works in the city of Corinth. You can see how the gospel penetrated all levels of society, with slaves, public officials, consuls, leaders of the empire, all sharing an equal ground of fellowship in the church of Jesus Christ.

Faithful Commitment

The thing we need to remember from this list of names is that these Christians were noted for their steady, tested commitment, their faithfulness to the gospel. I must say that I am troubled today when I see Christians succumbing so easily to the world's philosophy of life: live for your own pleasure, try to retire as early as possible so you can do as little as you can. I think that is a deadly philosophy. The early Christians did not believe that.

Four things ring clearly throughout their lives. *One*, they were not their own. They believed, as Paul wrote in 1 Corinthians 6:19 and 20, "You are not your own; you are bought with a price." They knew they did not have a right to direct their lives any longer. God had sent them into the world, and God would take them through it. *Second*, they believed that life is a battle, a battle to the death. It is not a picnic. They were engaged in warfare that never ended until they left this life, so they kept on fighting. *Third*, they believed that there is need for rest and leisure at times, but only to restore them to go back into the battle.

Finally (*fourth*), they understood that the gifts of the Holy Spirit among them opened up a ministry for every single believer. No Christian was without a ministry. Some of these dear people had only the gift of helps (although I should not say "only" the gift of helps, for that is a great gift.) They could not teach or preach but they could help, and they did, right to the end. Surely this passage reminds us that God has called us all to a ministry, and we all have to give an account for what we have done with our gifts. We had better find out what they are and get to work, because God has not called us to a picnic ground, but to a battle-ground.

17

The Great Mystery

Now we have come to the very last paragraph of the letter to the Romans. Probably at this point Paul took the pen
and wrote the final words in his own hand. He tells us in
2 Thessalonians that it was his custom to do this—to protect
his letters from forgery, for one thing—but also to bear a
personal greeting to those to whom he was writing. Almost
all scholars agree that the apostle probably suffered from a
serious eye problem, as the letter to the Galatians suggests.
So Paul wrote these marvelous words in large letters with
his own hand:

> Now to him who is able to establish you by my gospel and
> the proclamation of Jesus Christ, according to the revelation
> of the mystery hidden for long ages past, but now revealed
> and made known through the prophetic writings by the com-
> mand of the eternal God, so that all nations might believe and
> obey him—to the only wise God be glory forever through
> Jesus Christ! Amen (vv. 25–27).

Those remarkable words constitute a summary of the whole
letter to the Romans—a beautiful finale to this great epistle.
Notice that the goal the apostle has in view is that we who
read this letter may be established. Have you ever had the

desire to be established? Many people think they are established when actually they are simply stuck in the mud! Most of us think that being established means the end of all progress; we sit down, camp there, and that is it. In that sense, there are many Christians who are established. But when Paul speaks of our being established he means that we stand on solid, stable ground doctrinally and in experience.

Have you ever erected a picnic table outdoors and tried to find a place where all four legs touched the ground at the same time? You tried to establish it so that it would not rock, or become shaky. That is the idea Paul has in mind in this word "establish." God wants to bring you and me to a place where we are no longer rocking or shaky or unstable, but solid and secure. The idea is basically what all human beings look for: an inner security from which you can handle all the problems of life. You become dependable, and have a true sense of worth, so that nothing gets to you or shakes you up, or throws you off balance.

The One Who Is Able

Notice the resource that the apostle counts on to make that happen: "Now to him who is able to establish you. . . ." It is God himself who is responsible for this. You and I are not given the final responsibility to bring this about. Isn't that encouraging? Now there are things God asks us to do: We are to understand what he is saying to us in this letter and we are to cooperate with him and give ourselves to these things. But even if we do not, Paul is saying, we do not have the ultimate responsibility to bring this about. God will do it.

I am sure that as the apostle wrote this he had in mind all the instances and circumstances from the past that are given to us in the Old Testament to encourage us. God established Abraham, who was an idol worshiper. Abraham could not tell the truth about his wife. He was always lying about her because he thought that would save him from difficulty. Though Abraham had various character faults,

God stabilized him, established him, and brought him to
a place where he became one of the great names of all time.
God did this with Moses and David and, of course, with
Paul himself. Paul was a brilliant young Jew with an am-
bitious heart, a sharp mind, and a strong sense of achieve-
ment, due to his notable gifts and his desire to become
famous. Yet God broke him, softened him, changed him and
put him through circumstances that Paul did not understand
at the time. Finally he was established so that no matter
what came, he remained strong, steady, trusting, and certain.
That is the great good news of this letter. "Now to him who
is able to establish you. . . ."

Paul goes on to give us three things that God will use dur-
ing that process. *First* he says, "Now to him who is able to
establish you *by my gospel*. . . ." Now, do not misunder-
stand that little phrase. Paul does not mean by this that he
has a unique gospel. Unfortunately, some teachers have
taken these words in that way, and have concluded that
the apostle Paul was given a special revelation that no one
else possessed—one that Peter, James, John, and other writ-
ers of Scripture did not know. That teaching has been
widespread among certain men of our day, and many have
followed that delusion. That is not what Paul means. He
answered that accusation in 1 Corinthians when he said,
in effect, "Some of you are following me; some are following
Apollos; some are following Cephas, and this is wrong. We
are not different; we all have the same gospel. You are making too much of men. The message is always the same."
He rebuked them for tending to divide and to follow certain
leaders and teachers.

A Unique Revelation

What Paul means is that he was given a unique revelation
of this gospel. You find that in chapter 11 of 1 Corinthians:
"For I received from the Lord what I also passed on to you:
The Lord Jesus, on the night he was betrayed, took bread,
and when he had given thanks, he broke it and said, 'This

is my body, which is for you. . . .' " Paul is saying, "I was
not there at the Lord's supper. I was not even a Christian
then. I have not talked with Peter or James or John about
this, and none of the men who were present there told me
what happened in that room. I know what happened because Jesus himself appeared to me and told me. I have told
you only what I received from the Lord himself." The Lord
taught Paul the same gospel that the other apostles believed
and that is what Paul means when he says, "According to
my gospel."

The practical impact of this phrase upon us is this: the
test of all true Christian messages is that they be in line with
the apostolic writings. The apostles are the ones who tell
us the truth about the gospel. That is why we must always
check what we hear today that claims to be Christian and
see if it fits with what the apostles gave us. Paul says that
is what God will use to establish you: "My gospel, that
which was given to me."

The *second* element is the proclamation of Jesus Christ.
Here Paul is unfolding to us the heart of his gospel. Paul
was a mighty theologian; there has never been a greater.
Sometimes when I visit seminaries I am tempted to say to
the young men and women studying there, "Why waste your
time with these fourth-rate theologians of today, when you
could be spending your time with the first-rate theologians:
Peter, James, John, and Paul?" Theology was not the heart
of Paul's gospel, however. The heart of his gospel was the
revelation of a Person, Jesus himself. All through this letter
Paul has emphasized that fact again and again: everything
centers in Christ. He is the heart of it all. Therefore, a gospel
that leaves out Christ is a phony gospel. Jesus himself said,
"I am the way, the truth, and the life. No man comes to the
Father except by me." There Jesus declared the uniqueness
of his position. In the whole realm of theology there is no
one like Jesus Christ. In all the history of the religions of
the world, there is no one equal to him, or to be remotely
compared to him. Therefore, any gospel that minimizes
Christ, or puts him on the level of other names, is a perver-

sion of the true gospel of Jesus Christ. Christ is the central figure of all history, of all time, of all faith.

The Mystery Revealed

There is a *third* element, the apostle says, which has been the theme throughout Romans, although it is not always called by the same terms. Paul says, "God will use not only my gospel and the proclamation of Jesus Christ, but he will also establish you by the 'explanation of the mystery.'"

> . . . according to the revelation of the mystery hidden for long ages past, but now revealed and made known through the prophetic writings by the command of the eternal God, so that all nations might believe and obey him. . . .

Here is the mystery. The ultimate test of any Christian message is: does it proclaim the mystery? There are thousands of places in this land today where people meet regularly in Christian churches. They sing the same hymns we sing, and read the same Bible, and praise God in the same way. And yet, in thousands and thousands of those churches, nothing exciting is happening, nothing that reaches out and touches the community. Do you know why? Because the mystery is not being proclaimed. Here is the heart of the gospel, this amazing mystery. The question we need to ask about any church is, "Does it teach men and women to live on the basis of that fantastic secret, which was once hidden but is now fully revealed?"

What is this mystery? There are several references to it in the New Testament, sometimes referring to a part of it, sometimes referring to the whole. The only other reference to this mystery in the letter to the Romans is found in chapter 11:

> I do not want you to be ignorant of this mystery, brothers, so that you may not be conceited: [when Christians become conceited it is because they have forgotten the mystery] Israel has experienced a hardening in part until the full number of the

Gentiles has come in. And so all Israel will be saved, as it is written . . . (vv. 25,26).

That is part of the mystery. Paul is referring to the fact that God intends to unite both Jews and Gentiles into one body. For this to happen, the Jews must be partially blinded for a while, in order to allow the Gentiles to see. That is what has been going on for 2,000 years of human history: a partial blindness in Israel. We do not understand fully what is involved here, but it seems to be necessary in the program of God.

That aspect of the mystery is also referred to in Ephesians 3:2-6:

> Surely you have heard about the administration of God's grace that was given to me for you, that is, the mystery made known to me by revelation, as I have already written briefly. In reading this, then, you will be able to understand my insight into the mystery of Christ, which was not made known to man in other generations as it has been revealed by the Spirit to God's holy apostles and prophets. [The New Testament apostles and prophets.] This mystery is that through the gospel the Gentiles are heirs together with Israel, members together of one body, and sharers together in the promise of Christ Jesus.

Now that is an extremely important part of the mystery. But these references to parts of the mystery are not to be regarded as distinct and separate mysteries. They are all one, as we will see. The heart of the mystery is given to us in the opening chapter of Colossians. Here is one of the clearest statements on it:

> Now I rejoice in what was suffered for you, and I fill up in my flesh what is still lacking in regard to Christ's afflictions, for the sake of his body, which is the church. I have become its servant by the commission God gave me to present to you the word of God in its fullness—the mystery that has been kept hidden for ages and generations, but is now disclosed to the saints. To them God has chosen to make known among the Gentiles the glorious riches of this mystery, which is *CHRIST IN YOU, THE HOPE OF GLORY* (vv. 24-27 italics mine).

There is the mystery. All that God is, wrapped up in a Person, and given to you and to me—the only hope we have of ever discovering the glory that God intended for us as human beings. Christ *in you*, the hope of glory.

There is another reference to the wonder of this mystery in 1 Timothy 3:16. Paul describes it in terms of a hymn of the early church. He says,

Beyond all question, the mystery of godliness is great:

He appeared in a body,
    was vindicated by the Spirit,
was seen by angels,
    was preached among the nations,
was believed on in the world,
    was taken up in glory.

Jesus himself is the mystery. By means of the virgin birth of Jesus, by means of his holy, sinless life, by means of his substitutionary death upon a violent and cruel cross, by means of his startling break-out from the prison of death, and by means of the gift of the Holy Spirit on the day of Pentecost, God has given Jesus, all that he is and all that he has, to you and to me. This enables us to do two things: to deny our natural abilities and strengths, and to rely wholly on Jesus' ability and strength—and thus to live our lives today as though Jesus himself was living them. That is the mystery. That is the radical, powerful secret of authentic Christianity: Christ in you, the hope of glory.

Never Boring

Do you know that mystery? Do you know it not only in your mind but do you live it? It is the knowledge of it and the living of it that turns Christianity into an exciting adventure. It may be demanding, it may even be scary, but I can guarantee you one thing: it will never be boring, because the mystery is at work. If you are filled with the secret, the indwelling of Christ, it does not make any difference if you are a Jew or a Gentile. All the divisions of class, sex, and national origin are eliminated by that secret. It does not make any difference whether you are rich or poor, slave or free, all are one in Christ Jesus by that mystery. And whenever a Christian lives on that basis, really trusting the fact that God is in him through Jesus Christ to be his wisdom, his power, his strength; when he attempts things only on the basis of expecting God to fulfill his promise, and so he moves out to do things by God's grace, he finds himself "established." If you want a place of security it is not going to come by your reckoning on what you can do for God. That will never work. It is going to depend on how much you believe God is ready to do something through you.

Paul says two further things about this. *First,* though the results of this life style were *experienced* by men and women of God in the Old Testament, no *explanation* was ever given there of how this happened. When you read the Old Testament you find men and women puzzled as to how God was going to put together all its great promises and themes. There is the promise of the restoration of Israel. There is also the promise of the forgiveness of an individual's sins. And there is the mighty promise of the healing of the nations and the cessation of war. At last the process of fulfilment began to unfold; Jesus came. He was the secret. He would be the One who would fulfill all the tremendous promises and themes of the Old Testament. Therefore, the historic appearance of Jesus was required to put this victorious life style in such vivid light that it could be preached and demonstrated to the nations of the world. That is what Paul means when he says that the mystery was "hidden for long ages past, but now revealed." It was experienced before; it was explained by the coming of Jesus.

The *second* thing Paul says is that it was "made known through the prophetic writings by the command of the eternal God." This is a reference to the New Testament as we have it today. The apostles and prophets wrote the gospel down for us so that we might have a clear picture of

who Jesus is, and what he can be in us. This is why we must
study the New Testament particularly (and the Old Testament as well), so we can understand how to live on the
basis of the mystery.

Now Paul closes with a great doxology.

—to the only wise God be glory forever through Jesus Christ!
Amen.

What a plan! What a program! Let us renew our commitment to fulfill that mystery not only at church, but in every
situation we face throughout the week. Every moment of
pressure and every demand upon us are simply opportunities to realize again the validity of the mystery—Christ in
you, the hope of glory.

A Detailed Outline of Romans

I. From Guilt to Glory—Explained, chaps. 1–8

    A. Introduction: The Themes of Romans 1:1–17

        1. Jesus Christ, our Lord, 1–6

            a. Promised beforehand by the prophets, 1,2

            b. Presented by the Spirit, 3,4

                (1) as "the sperm of David," 3

                (2) as the Son of God (by the resurrection), 4

            c. Present in history, 5,6

                (1) One who chose Paul, 5

                (2) One who called the Romans, 6

        2. The Saints of God (at Rome and elsewhere), 7–12

            a. Called, 7

                (1) Originates in God's love

                (2) Continues by grace and peace

            b. Active in faith, 8

            c. Supported by prayer, 9,10

            d. Strengthened by gifts, 11,12

        3. The Apostle Paul, 13–15

            a. His ambition, 13

            b. His obligation, 14

            c. His anticipation, 15

        4. The Gospel, 16,17

            a. Its effect—makes me "not ashamed," 16

            b. Its nature, 16,17

           (1) to manifest the power of God

           (2) to reveal the righteousness of God

      c. Its channel—by faith, 17

           (1) "everyone who believes"

           (2) whether Jew or Gentile

B. THE NEED FOR THE GOSPEL, 1:18–3:20

    1. *The universal wrath of God, 18–32*

        a. Its inescapability—revealed from heaven, 18

        b. Its cause, 18

           (1) the godlessness of men

           (2) the wickedness of men—suppression of truth

        c. The truth men suppress, 19,20

           (1) The existence of God

           (2) Made plain in nature

               (a) His eternal power and majesty

               (b) Everywhere and in every age

           (3) No excuse remains

        d. How men suppress the truth, 21–23

           (1) They ignore God, 21

               (a) The means—no glory, no thanks

               (b) The effect—futile thinking, darkened hearts

           (2) They imitate God, 22

               (a) How?—They claim to be wise

               (b) The effects—Become fools

           (3) They insult God, 23

               (a) How?—Make images of God

               (b) Effects—Wickedness

        e. The nature of wrath, 24–32

           (1) God gave them over—to sexual license, 24

               (a) Bodies are degraded

               (b) Immorality becomes widely acceptable

           (2) God gave them over—to homosexuality, 25–27

               (a) Exchanged truth for a lie, 25

               (b) Exchanged natural for unnatural, 26,27

               (c) Received due penalty—loss of psychological identity

           (3) God gave them over—to cruel depravity, 28–32

               (a) Widespread violence, 28–31

               (b) Shameless defiance, 32

    2. *The Sinfully Moral, 2:1–13*

        a. Those who pass judgment on others, 1–5

  (1) Condemn themselves, 1
    (a) Because obviously know wrong from right
    (b) Yet do the same things (inwardly)
  (2) Deceive themselves, 2–4a
    (a) God of truth will overlook, 2
    (b) God of patience will forget, 3–4a
  (3) Store up wrath for themselves, 4b,5
    (a) God's kindness received leads to repentance
    (b) God's kindness rejected stores up wrath

b. God's principles of judgment, 6–11
  (1) Patiently waits till "works" appear, 6–8
    (a) If truly want glory and honor and immortality—show by patience in well–doing eternal life) receive Christ
    (b) If inwardly factious and wicked—show by not obeying truth (reject Christ)—wrath
  (2) Disregards all national or racial advantages
    (a) To evil Jews or Gentiles—tribulation, 9–11
    (b) To good Jews or Gentiles—glory, honor, peace
  (3) Uses individual's own standard, 12,13
    (a) Those who do not know law—perish without
    (b) Those who do know law—If *do* it.

3. *The unenlightened pagans, 14–16*
a. Have a law written on their hearts, 14,15
  (1) Moral deeds prove this
  (2) Conscience judges them
b. Results in restlessness, 16
  (1) alternating fear and momentary appeasement
  (2) conscience cannot remove guilt
c. Revealed in day of judgment, 16

4. *The religious moralist, 2:17–3:8 (Jew)*
a. Has impressive advantages, 17,18
  (1) possesses the law
  (2) has a relationship with God
  (3) knows will of God
  (4) approves what is excellent
  (5) instructed by law
b. Performs significant activities, 19,20
  (1) guide to the blind
  (2) light to the darkened

        (3) instructor of foolish

        (4) teacher of children

  c. But guilty of blasphemous hypocrisy, 20–24

        (1) Oversharp in business (stole)

        (2) Immoral with slave girls (adultery)

        (3) Trafficked with pagan temples (idolatry)

        (4) Broke law 1,001 ways (lawless)

        (5) Turned off many (blasphemy)

  d. Relies on outward ritual, 25–29

        (1) Circumcision, without obedience, rejected

        (2) Uncircumcision, with obedience, received

        (3) Righteousness without rite better than rite without righteousness (Subst. baptism)

        (4) Jewishness is matter of faith—not fanaticism

  e. Jewish objections answered, 3:1–8

        (1) Will you eliminate the advantages God gave? 1,2

           (a) no—truly great advantages

           (b) but if not used—worthless

        (2) If *some* fail, will all be lost? 3,4

           (a) no—man fails, God does not, 4

           (b) David an example

        (3) If sin gives God opportunity, how can he condemn? 5–8

           (a) on that basis, no one judged, 6

           (b) Paul's personal example, 7,8

              —eliminates dif. between good and evil

              —expects good out of evil

5. *Man's universal condition (total wipeout),* 9–20

  a. Already demonstrated—all under sin, 9

        (1) Gentiles:

           (a) blatantly wicked defy God

           (b) morally self–righteous delude themselves

           (c) darkened pagan defiles his conscience

        (2) Jew: denies in deed what teaches in word

  b. Confirmed by Scripture, 10–18

        (1) The *character* of men, 10–12

        (2) The *conduct* of men, 13–17

           (a) their speech, 13,14

           (b) their deeds, 15–17

  c. The work of law, 19,20

        (1) Shut men's mouths

   (2) Hold all accountable

   (3) Bring to justification because of knowledge of sin

C. The Gift of Righteousness, 3:21–31

 1. What is God's answer to man's failure? 21

  a. The righteousness (worth) of God

  b. Given apart from law

  c. Witnessed to by the prophets

   (1) They possessed it

   (2) They describe it

 2. How is it obtained? 22–24

  a. Through faith in Jesus Christ (His person and work)

  b. For all who believe (not automatic)

  c. Without distinction (no partiality)

  d. By a gracious gift (God's work)

  e. Through redemption (death and resurrection of Christ)

 3. How redemption works, 25a

  a. A propitiatory blood sacrifice

   (1) expiation—satisfies justice

   (2) propitiation—releases love

 4. Why redemption provided, 25b,26

  a. To vindicate God, 25b,26

   (1) His justice questioned because of past forbearance

   (2) Now his long-delayed punishment falls on Jesus

  b. To justify those who believe, 26b

 5. The results of the gift of righteousness, 27–31

  a. No one can boast, 27,28

  b. No one is excluded, 29,30

  c. Law is upheld, 31

D. Abraham—A Man Made Righteous by Faith, 4:1–25

 1. The father of faith, 1–12

  a. How was Abraham made righteous? 1–8

   (1) One possibility—performance, 1,2

    (a) boast before men

    (b) worthless before God

   (2) What he did—believed God, 3

    (a) believed about coming seed

    (b) credited to him as righteousness

   (3) An illustration from life, 4,5

    (a) work *earns* payment

    (b) Abraham given a gift—righteousness

        (4) An illustration from Scripture, 6–8
           (a) David was immoral and guilty
           (b) yet given gift of righteousness
    b. When was Abraham made righteous? 9–11a
        (1) Before he was circumcised, 9,10
           (a) 14 years after declared righteous
           (b) no saving value in ritual
        (2) Circumcision had another purpose, 11a
           (a) sign, to remind
           (b) seal, to guarantee
    c. Why was Abraham made righteous? 11b,12
        (1) To make him a father
           (a) of all uncircumcised who have righteousness by believing, 11b
           (b) of all circumcised who are made righteous by faith, 12
        (2) We are all children of Abraham by faith
2. *The faith of our father, 13–25*
    a. What faith is not. Not trying to keep the law, 13–15
        (1) Promise to Abraham not associated with law, 13
        (2) To add condition after a promise disannuls promise, 14
        (3) Conditions of the law only produces wrath, 15
    b. What faith does, 16,17a
        (1) Allows the promise to rest on grace, 16
        (2) Guarantees it to all Abraham's descendants, 17a
    c. How faith works, 17b–22
        (1) Relies on the character of its object, 17b
           (a) a God who gives life to the dead
           (b) a God who calls into existence things that do not exist
        (2) Faces all obstacles squarely, 18–20a
           (a) hopeless circumstances, 18,19
               —Abraham's dead body
               —Sarah's barren womb
           (b) staggering possibilities, 20a
        (3) Acts in line with invisible realities, 20b–22
           (a) grew strong in faith, 20b
           (b) gave glory to God, 21
           (c) grasped the promise, 22

      d. Who faith benefits, 23–25

        (1) Helped Abraham—friend of God

        (2) Helps us—frees from guilt, grants us worth

E. THE RESULTS OF RIGHTEOUSNESS—REJOICING, 5:1–21

    1. Rejoicing in our spiritual position, 1,2

      a. Sense of complete assurance—peace with God

      b. Provision for constant supply—access by grace

      c. Hope of confident anticipation—share glory of God

    2. Rejoicing in our present sufferings, 3–10

      a. The Christian response to trouble

      b. The reasons why we rejoice, 3,4

        (1) Knowing suffering produces

          (a) endurance (steadiness)

          (b) character (reliability)

          (c) hope (present awareness)

          (d) does not disappoint (boldness)

        (2) Comes because of love of God, 5–8

          (a) time when we felt unlovable, helpless, ungodly, sinners, enemies

          (b) yet in cross saw loved

          (c) if then, surely loved now, 9,10

    3. Rejoicing in our mighty Redeemer, 11–21

      a. Where we began "in Adam," 11–14

        (1) Sin and death came through one man, 12

        (2) Death proves the fact of sin, 13,14

          (a) even before the law

          (b) even over "innocents"

      b. The greater parallel "in Christ," 15–19

        (1) Adam's trespass brought a single experience of death to all in him. Christ brings a repeated and ever-growing experience of life to all in him (abounds), 15

        (2) One trespass of Adam produced condemnation (guilt) in all. Many trespasses are wiped out by justification in Christ, 16

        (3) Because of Adam, death *reigned* over all men. Because of Jesus Christ, all who receive grace and righteousness *reign* in life now, 17

        (4) Guilt not earned by individuals—it is the gift of Adam. Forgiveness & life not earned either—it is the gift of Christ, 18

(5) To sin is not an option for those in Adam—it is inevitable. To be righteous is not an option for those in Christ—it is inevitable, 19

  c. The parallel between law and grace, 20,21

    (1) Law did its work

      (a) increased trespass

      (b) made sin reign by *death*

    (2) Grace overflowed

      (a) reigned through gift of righteousness

      (b) to produce eternal life *through Jesus Christ*

F. THE PROBLEM OF LICENSE, 6:1–23

  1. Can we go on practicing sin? 1–14

    a. Absolutely not, 1,2

      (1) We died to sin

      (2) How *can* we live in it?

    b. The figure of baptism, 3,4

      (1) Died by means of the Spirit's baptism

      (2) Involved death, burial, and resurrection

      (3) For one purpose—newness of life

    c. The figure of grafting, 5

      (1) His death accomplished our death

      (2) His resurrection made us alive

    d. The effect of death & burial, 6,7

      (1) "Old man" was crucified

        (a) the essential you—human spirit

        (b) Adamic life ended

      (2) "Body of sin" rendered controllable

        (a) sin located in bodies

        (b) power over body broken in dying of Jesus

      (3) No longer a slave to sin

    e. The effect of resurrection, 8–10

      (1) Ressurection power takes us beyond death, 8,9

      (2) Resurrection is God living in us, 10

    f. Two steps to follow, 11–13 (1st exhortation)

      (1) Refuse sin's right to use your body, 12,13a

      (2) Return your members to God for his use, 13b

    g. You'll win! 14

      (1) Law provides no way back

      (2) Grace makes possible instant recovery

  2. Should we permit ourselves occasional sin? 15–23

    a. Absolutely not, 15

    b. Because sin makes you a slave, 16–19
        (1) Man is meant to be mastered, 16
        (2) There is no *necessity* to be a slave to sin, 17,18
        (3) Claim your right to live righteously, 19
    c. Because sin makes you ashamed, 20,21a
        (1) Your past experience proves it
        (2) What value to you is there in shame?
    d. Because sin brings death into your experience, 21b–23
        (1) There is no escaping death when you sin
        (2) Why not choose life?
G. The Problem of Legalism, 7:1–8:2
    1. *How we now relate to the law, 7:1–6*
        a. The illustration from marriage, 1–3
            (1) The point: law is for the living, not the dead
            (2) The factors: a woman; first and second husbands; the law
            (3) The argument:
                (a) law demands a woman remain with her husband, or be stigmatized (adulteress)
                (b) only when her husband dies is she free to remarry—law is then silent, 2b,3b
        b. The analogy to life, 4–6
            (1) You (the woman) are free from the law, 4a
                (a) "body of Christ" is Christ, made sin for us
                (b) when he died, woman discharged from law
            (2) You (the woman) free to marry another, 4b
                (a) Christ, raised from the dead
                (b) so we can bear fruit for God
            (3) The contrasting conditions, 5,6
                (a) with husband #1 (the flesh)—fruit for death
                (b) with husband #2 (the Spirit)—new life
    2. *How the law arouses sin and "kills" us—explained, 7–13*
        a. Paul's experience before a Christian, 7–11
            (1) Law helped him discover his sin, 7
            (2) When confronted with law, sin was aroused, 8a
            (3) Once he had no sense of sin, 8b–11
                (a) raised in sheltered, godly home
                (b) exposed to opportunity—felt force of law
                (c) precipitated orgy of covetousness
        b. Is the law, then, evil? 12,13
            (1) No, it is sin that brings death, 12,13a

(2) Law reveals sin as exceedingly sinful, 13b

3. *How the law arouses sin and "kills" us—experienced, 7:14–8:2*

    a. Paul's experience as a Christian, 14–25

        (1) Carnal—sold as a slave, 14 (comp. 6:17)

        (2) Finds two problems, 16–23

            (a) problems stated, 15

            (b) "If I do what I do not want" 16–20

                [1] something in me agrees law is good, 16

                [2] but something else (sin) makes me do bad, 17

                [3] my will is right, but sin is stronger, 18,19

                [4] so my true self (spirit) not the culprit, 20

            (c) "I do not do what I want" 21–24

                [1] when I want to do right—sin right there, 21

                [2] my spirit delights in law, but sin wins, 22–23

                [3] result is wretchedness and cry of frustration, 24

        (3) The glorious answer, 7:25–8:1

            (a) the law cannot help but Christ does, 25a

            (b) despite my struggle I am not condemned, 26–8:1

    b. The principle of freedom, 8:2

H. Newness of Life, 8:2–17

    1. *Review of basis for victory, 2–4*

        a. Law powerless to help, 3a

        b. Son came to enable, 3b

            (1) in the flesh, but not sinful

            (2) dealt with sin in the flesh (by death)

            (3) imparted the righteousness law required

        c. All available to those who choose the Spirit, 4

    2. *The two choices described, 5–13*

        a. Two focuses of concern, 5

            (1) things of the flesh

            (2) things of the Spirit

        b. Two inescapable results, 6

            (1) death (fear, guilt, hostility, emptiness)

            (2) life and peace (trust, security, love, well-being)

      c. Two reasons, 7
         (1) flesh hostile to God (stated)
         (2) Spirit pleasing to God (implied)
   3. *The two kinds of men, 8,9 (parenthetical)*
      a. "In the flesh"—without the Spirit, 8b
      b. "In the Spirit"—Spirit indwells, 9
   4. *Two abiding facts about the Christian, 10,11*
      a. Bodies dying but spirits alive, 10
      b. Dying bodies can serve God, through the Spirit, 11
   5. *One obligation, 12,13*
      a. Can live by the flesh, but about to die
      b. Only obligation—live by the Spirit, 13
   6. *The sons of God, 14–17*
      a. How can know you are a son, 14,15
         (1) Because led by Spirit of God, 14
            (a) became a son by adoption
            (b) not a slave but a son
         (2) Because you cry "Abba Father," 16
            (a) comes from Spirit's witness within
            (b) expresses itself in child's cry
      b. Sonship also involves heirship, 17
         (1) Not only heir of world, but heir of universe
         (2) Linked with suffering
I. Incomparable Glory Ahead, 18–25
   1. *The glory vastly exceeds the suffering, 18*
      a. In intensity
      b. In locality
   2. *Nature testifies to the coming glory, 19–22*
      a. Nature is waiting for something, 19
      b. Since it fell with man, it will be freed with man, 20,21
      c. It now groans in hope, 22
   3. *Our present experience confirms this, 23–25*
      a. Believers also groan, 23
      b. But we groan in hope, 24,25
         (1) salvation includes the body
         (2) we wait, therefore, with patience
J. The Place of Prayer, 26–28
   1. *What shall we ask God for? 26,27*
      a. Lack wisdom to know
      b. Lack words to ask
      c. Spirit helps by unutterable groans

      2. *The Father's answer to the Spirit's prayer, 28*

  K. GOD'S GREAT PURPOSE AND OUR PROPER RESPONSE, 29–39

      1. *The purpose of God—conformed to Christ's image, 29,30*

         a. Those whom he foreknew

         b. He also predestined

         c. These he also called

         d. These he also justified

         e. These he also glorified (where is sanctified?)

      2. *What then shall we say? 31–39*

         a. "If God is for us, who is against us?" 31,32

            (1) removes fear of opposition

            (2) removes fear of lack

         b. "Who shall bring any charge against God's elect?" 33,34

            (1) because of justification, no accusation possible

            (2) because of sanctification, no condemnation

         c. "Who shall separate us from love of Christ?" 35–39

            (1) circumstances of life, 35–37

            (2) powers within and beyond life, 38,39

II. From Guilt to Glory—Exhibited, chapters 9–11

  A. PAUL'S GREAT SORROW. 9:1–3

      1. *Hurt is real, 1*

         a. Conscience supports

         b. Holy Spirit confirms

      2. *Hurt is deep and lasting, 2,3*

         a. Continual, 2

         b. Sacrificial, 3

  B. ISRAEL'S GREAT FAILURE, 4,5

      1. *Their past advantages, 4,5a*

         a. The adoption

         b. The glory (Shekinah)

         c. The covenants

         d. The law

         e. The worship

         f. The promises

         g. The patriarchs

      2. *Their present supreme opportunity: Divine Messiah*

  C. GOD'S GREAT FAITHFULNESS, 6–18

      1. *His principles of selection, 6–13*

         a. Never based on natural advantages, 6,7

            (1) not all descendants of Jacob (Israel)

    (2) not all descendants of Abraham
   b. Always based on a promise, 8,9
    (1) Ishmael excluded—son of the flesh
    (2) Isaac chosen—came by promise
   c. Never based on human works, 10–13
    (1) Jacob and Esau had same father
    (2) neither babe had opportunity to work
  2. *Conclusion: election is God's sovereign choice, 14–18*
   a. Declared to Moses, 14,15
   b. Demonstrated in Pharaoh, 16,17
   c. Described by Paul, 18
 D. Man's Objection Answered, 19–29
  1. *Objection stated: God makes us sin and then condemns us for sinning, 19*
  2. *Objection answered: 20–29*
   a. Let's examine your credentials, 20
   b. Even men exert a form of sovereignty, 21
   c. Consider two possible motives in God's choice, 22–28
    (1) his wrath, power, and patience made known by disobedience of men, 22
    (2) his wrath displayed brought ones he chose to him to learn riches of glory, 23
     (a) Gentiles saved, on this basis
     (b) Hosea and Isaiah predicted
   d. No one saved if no election, 29
  3. *Evident conclusion, 30–33*
   a. Ignorant and sinful Gentiles made righteous—through faith, 30
   b. Zealous and privileged Jews failed—because of works, 31,32
   c. How you can tell God's elect—what do with Jesus, 33
    (1) non-elect stumble
    (2) elect believe and stand
 E. How to Be Saved, 10:1–13 (Note verses 1 and 13)
  1. *Israel's failure, 1–4*
   a. Though Paul yearned and prayed for it, 1
   b. And the Jews zealously desired it, 2
   c. They missed it because of ignorance, 3
   d. Since they clung to law and rejected Christ, 4
  2. *The steps of salvation, 5–9*
   a. Realize perfect righteousness necessary, 5 (Moses)

        b. Give up all hope of arranging it yourself, 6,7 (Moses)

        c. Understand God's announcement has reached you, 8

        d. Acknowledge that Jesus is Lord, 9a

        e. Believe in his resurrected presence, 9b

    3. *The explanation of it, 10*

        a. God sees the heart belief and gives righteousness, 10a

        b. Man confesses his willing surrender—saved

    4. *The availability of it, 11–13*

        a. Open to all who believe

        b. Open to all who call

  F. GOD'S EFFORTS TO REACH MEN, 10:14–31

    1. *What lies behind men's call? 14,15*

        a. To call, must believe

        b. To believe, must hear

        c. To hear, there must be a preacher

        d. To preach, there must be a Sender (beautiful and welcome)

    2. *The puzzle of unbelief, 16–21*

        a. Isaiah experienced it (Isaiah 53), 16

        b. Jesus is the issue! 17

        c. An inescapable proclamation, 18

        d. Provided with clear examples, 19,20

           (1) Moses—people with less intelligence believe, 19

           (2) Isaiah—people with less drive and desire, 20

        e. God beseeches with patient love, 21

  G. ISRAEL'S HOPE, 11:1–32

    1. *Jews are not rejected as individuals, 1–6*

        a. Paul an example, 1,2

           (1) one of those God "foreknew"

           (2) came through struggle and pain

        b. What Elijah forgot! 3–6

           (1) man's limited knowledge, 4

           (2) God's unlimited power, 5

           (3) two contrasting principles, 6

    2. *Yet unbelief results in hardening, 7–10*

        a. Isaiah—won't understand; won't heed, 8

        b. David—their hunger led to slavery, 9,10

    3. *Why Israel will yet become a godly nation, 11–24 (Goebbels)*

        a. Salvation of Gentiles intended to arouse Israel, 11

         b. Worldwide blessing only when Israel returns, 12–15

      c. Abraham's blessing foresaw Israel's return, 16

      d. Gentiles, when saved, become children of Abraham, 17–21

      e. Believing Jews more naturally sons of God, 22–24

    4. *The prediction of Israel's return, 25–29*

      a. A humbling mystery, 25

        (1) a hardening *in part*, 25a

        (2) limited in duration—"until," 25b

        (3) revealed to prevent Gentile conceit

      b. All Israel will be saved, 26,27

        (1) the Deliverer will begin in Jerusalem, 26a

        (2) he will end Jewish unbelief, 26b

        (3) he will forgive their sins, 27

      c. Two present implications, 28,29

        (1) they may treat you as enemies, 28a

        (2) yet they are loved by an unchanging God, 29

    5. *God's "wheels within wheels," 30–32*

      a. Uses Jewish disobedience to give opportunity to rebellious Gentiles to find mercy, 30

      b. Then uses Gentile mercies to make Jews jealous so they can receive mercy, 31

      c. Concludes that awareness of disobedience necessary step to salvation, 32

  H. The Greatness of God, 33–36

    1. *God's inscrutable wisdom and ways, 33*

      a. judgments beyond accountability

      b. ways beyond understanding

    2. *The contrasting impotence of man, 34,35*

      a. Who has ever second-guessed God? 34a

      b. Who has suggested something God never thought of? 34b

      c. Who has given God something he never had? 35

    3. *The Originator, Sustainer, and Finisher of all, 36*

III. **From Guilt to Glory—Experienced, chapters 12–16**

  A. God's Strategy to Change the World, 12:1–13:14

    1. *Start with yourself, 12:1,2*

      a. Bring your *bodies* to God, 1

        (1) your response to his loving acts

        (2) make it a daily commitment (living sacrifice)

        (3) know that God is pleased and comfortable

        (4) only reasonable and logical thing to do

   b. Challenge the culture of the age, 2a
     (1) recognize its mistaken concepts
     (2) resist its subtle pressures
   c. Keep correcting your thinking, 2b
     (1) mental adjustment
     (2) spiritual refreshment
   d. Demonstrate the practical character of God's will, 2c
   e. Take inventory of your abilities, 3
     (1) don't overrate yourself
     (2) observe the limits of self-appraisal
     (3) remember God's balance

2. *Put your gifts to work in the church, 4–13*
   a. God's great visual aid—your body, 4,5
     (1) diversity function
     (2) unity of life
   b. A sampling of gifts, 6–8
     (1) speaking gifts
       (a) prophesying
       (b) teaching
       (c) exhorting
     (2) serving gifts
       (a) service
       (b) contributions
       (c) leadership
       (d) showing mercy
   c. Love—among Christians, 9–13
     (1) hates sin; accepts persons, 9
     (2) bases love on relationship—not friendship, 10a
     (3) honors others above yourself, 10b
     (4) keeps enthusiastic—through the Lord, 11
     (5) rejoices in hope, 12
     (6) responds to needs, 13

3. *Carry your love into the world, 14–21*
   a. Speak well of your persecutors, 14
   b. Adjust to others' moods, 15
   c. Do not show partiality, 16
   d. Do not take a silent revenge, 17
   e. Seek to avoid strife, 18
   f. Renounce trying to get even, 10–21
     (1) God is already avenging, 19a
     (2) God claims sole right to avenge, 19b
     (3) something you can do, 20,21

      4. *Recognize the functions of government, 13:1–7*
         a. Where do governments originate? 1
            (1) God chooses the form
            (2) God selects the incumbents
         b. Rebellion against lawful government—rebellion against God, 2
         c. The legitimate powers of government, 3,4 and 6
            (1) protect from evil and provide special services
            (2) have two special powers
         d. The proper Christian response, 5 and 7
            (1) a respectful attitude, 5
            (2) a cheerful obedience, 7
      5. *Remember two central things, 8–13*
         a. The power of love, 8–10
            (1) see it as a debt, 8a
            (2) pay it to everyone, 8b
            (3) thus, fulfill the law, 9,10
         b. The nature of the present age, 11–14
            (1) time to wake up, 11,12a
            (2) time to give up, 12b,13
            (3) time to put on, 14
   B. How to Handle Differing Christian Convictions, 14:1–15:13
      1. *What you must not do, 1–12*
         a. Do not exclude weak brethren, 1
            (1) they belong to Christ (in the faith)
            (2) must not be argued out of doubts
         b. The two parties: freedom vs. limitation, 2,3
            (1) strong must not isolate weak
            (2) weak must not condemn strong
         c. Reason why, 4–12
            (1) not your responsibility to change brother in this area, 4
               (a) he is not your servant
               (b) Lord already changing
               (c) Lord well able to do it
            (2) God can read hearts and you cannot, 5–8
               (a) differences represent honest convictions, 5
               (b) God accepts both as honoring him, 6
               (c) your relationship more important that issue, 7,8
            (3) Christ alone won right to judge, 9–12

        (a) has both died and lived, 9

        (b) both strong and weak must give account, 10–12

2. *What you can do, 13–23*

    a. Decide never deliberately to stumble a brother, 13–15

        (1) conscience may be restraining him, 14

        (2) there are more important matters in life, 15

    b. Observe certain guidelines, 19–21

        (1) when threatens peace of church—give up

        (2) when angers or offends an individual so as to prevent investigation and growth, stop

    c. Base your own convictions only on the Word, 22,23

        (1) you will have an untroubled conscience

        (2) you will please God by your faith

3. *Our Great Example, 15:1–13*

    a. Christ did not please himself, 1–3

        (1) so strong should yield to the weak

            (a) if it is for his good

            (b) if it edifies him

    b. Encouragement from the past, 4

    c. Encouragement from the present, 5,6

    d. Encouragement from the future, 7–12

        (1) God is even reconciling Jews and Gentiles

        (2) began when Christ accepted both, despite differences

        (3) did it by not pleasing himself (ministry of circumcision)

        (4) so reached both Jews and Gentiles. to glory of God

            (a) truthfulness to Jews—mercy to Gentiles

            (b) two shall be one as scriptures predict

    e. So possibility of working these things out, 13

C. THE CHARACTER OF PAUL'S MINISTRY, *14–33*

   1. *His ministry to the saints at Rome, 14–16*

    a. To evaluate what they had, 14

        (1) right motives (full of goodness)

        (2) complete knowledge

        (3) full range of gifts (able to counsel)

    b. To supply what they lacked, 15,16

        (1) a bold reminder

        (2) a priestly ministry

        (3) a divine acceptance

2. *His ministry in other places, 17–33*
   a. Its secret of success, 17,18
   b. Its manifestation—power, 19a
   c. Its geographical extent, 19b
   d. Its uniqueness—pioneering, 20,21
3. *His present plans and ministry, 22–29*
   a. His long-felt desire to come to Rome, 22–24
   b. His immediate commitment to Jerusalem, 25–27
      (1) with material aid
      (2) to fulfill a spiritual principle
   c. His confidence of an effective ministry in Rome, 28,29
4. *His reliance on prayer, 30–33*
   a. His ground of expectation, 30
      (1) their obedience to their Lord
      (2) their share of love by the Spirit
   b. The nature of prayer—striving
   c. His specific requests, 31
      (1) to be delivered from unbelievers
      (2) to be accepted by the saints
      (3) to come with joy and share refreshment
D. The Circle of Paul's Friends, 16:1–24
   1. *Greetings to brothers and sisters in Rome, 1–16*
      a. Bearer of letter—Phoebe, 1–16
      b. Well-known husband and wife team, 3,4a
      c. Two cherished friends, 5b,6
      d. Some relatives and close friends, 7–10a
      e. Two groups of Christians and non-Christians, 10b,11
      f. Three hard-working ladies, 12
      g. An old friend with a fascinating history, 13
      h. A business man's group from Greece, 14
      i. Another house church, 15,16
   2. *Warning about false Christians, 17–20*
      a. Their danger: 17
         (1) create factions
         (2) erect obstacles to faith
      b. Their motives: 18a
         (1) not Christ
         (2) their own appetites
      c. Their methods: 18b
         (1) smooth words and flattery
         (2) work with simple-minded (naive)

       d. The way to handle them, 19,20
         (1) avoid them
         (2) ignore their teachings
         (3) God will handle them
    3. *Greetings from those with Paul, 21–24*
      a. His traveling companions, 21
      b. His local secretary and brother—Tertius, Quartus
      c. His host in Corinth, 23
      d. His prominent friend, Erastus
  E. THE GLORIOUS MYSTERY, 25–27
    1. *What is the mystery? 25*
      a. "My gospel and the preaching of Jesus Christ"
      b. Has power to strengthen
    2. *How did it come to us, 25b,26*
      a. Experienced by faith in the past, but not explained
      b. Now made known by prophetic writings
      c. In response to God's command
      d. To produce obedience of faith
    3. *Doxology, 27*